SWAHILI STYLE

Published in 2005 by:

Gallery Publications

P.O. Box 3181, Zanzibar

email: gallery@swahilicoast.com

© 2005 Gallery Publications

Photographs © Javed Jafferji

Text by Elie Losleben

Graphic Designer: Terence Fernandes

Designed by Zanzibar Gallery Publishers

Photographs are available for commercial use from Impact Photos in the UK

e mail: library@impactphotos.com

ISBN 9987 667 44 9

This book is dedicated to my son Kumail, who was born when I started this project.

Delicate henna paintings create intricate designs on a Moroccan lampshade at Kinasi Lodge.

SWAHILI STYLE

Javed Jafferji • Elie Losleben

Published by Gallery Publications

CONTENTS

Left: Lights and lanterns at Kiwandani House cast a magical glow across the pool and garden of the Moon Houses in Lamu.

Next page: A rooftop deck chair soaks up the sun at Beach House in Lamu.

Previous page: Hanging beds covered in *kangas* create a colourful place to lounge at Kipungani Explorer on Lamu Island.
Left: A *makuti* umbrella set against the deserted beach at Kipungani Explorer.
Right: A *dhow* in the quiet bay between Munira's Camp on Kiwayu Island and the mangrove creek.

Left: Mediterranean meets Swahili style at the entrace to Alfajiri's Clifftop Villa.
Right: Frangipani flowers complement the deep blue mosaic tiles at The Palms' pool
in Zanzibar.

Introduction

The Swahili Coast. Its name conjures up the minarets and narrow streets of old stone towns, the scent of spices roasting on an enclosed balcony, the full sails of trading *dhows* drifting on the evening breeze. Merchants and sailors have returned here for more than a thousand years, mooring their wooden boats in the archipelagos and natural harbours of the thousand-kilometre stretch of coastline between southern Somaliland and northern Mozambique. *Swahili Style* is a discovery of the traditions of the East African coast, investigating the many threads that make the tapestry of Swahili culture so rich in colour and alluring in detail. The meeting of African and Arab culture, the arrival of European explorers and Indian merchants, the slow blending of style, language and traditions from around the Indian Ocean – all worked to create a beautiful way of life and a sumptuous way of living.

Swahili Style goes inside the houses and hotels of Lamu, Mombasa, Zanzibar, Mafia and Dar es Salaam. We explore private retreats, elegant hotels, remote beach properties and restored stone houses to capture the aesthetic of the explorers and traders that centuries ago made the East African coast their home. We discover the best of Swahili architecture and design to offer a glimpse of life and leisure in the old stone towns, islands and beaches of Kenya, Tanzania and Zanzibar.

For millennia, the stretch of pristine coastline along eastern Africa has been the continent's point of contact with the outside world, a place of discoveries and meetings, shared traditions and trade. As early as the second century A.D., the ancient seafarers' handbook *Periplus of the Erithrean Sea* describes a scattering of ports along the Swahili Coast, referring in Greek to the Lamu Archipelago and describing the ivory trade in the town of Rhapta, whose location still remains unknown. "There are brought to these parts of Azania things made specially in

---

Left: A sumptuous couch accentuates an elaborate plaster wall niche in Baytil Ajaib.

southern Arabia," wrote the ancient mariner, "spears, axes, small swords, awls and several kinds of glassware. Exported from here are quantities of ivory, as well as rhino horn, tortoiseshell and pearly seashells." By the 9th century, permanent trading settlements in the Lamu Archipelago and in Mafia and Kilwa further south created a constant supply of gold, slaves and ivory in high demand all over the Indian Ocean. Gradually, a distinctly Swahili civilisation came into existence, one whose aesthetic drew from Arab, Indian and Bantu African roots to create a purely distinct culture with its own language, musical styles, oral history and literature.

From the 11th century to the 15th century, the feudal city-states that made up the trading networks of the Swahili Coast thrived and prospered under independent rule. In the great towns of Kilwa and Mogadishu, and the archipelagos of Lamu and Zanzibar, merchant families built lavish houses of coral and limestone, creating the first 'stone towns' of the Swahili Coast. A cosmopolitan urban layout based loosely upon the concept of the Arabian *medina* came into being, the towns' winding streets shaded from the tropical sun by tall whitewashed buildings adorned with carved doors and ornately carved plaster. Inside the stone houses, traditional features and local innovation combined to create comfortable retreats protected from sun and tropical elements. Stone mosques were also built in the centre of stone towns as focal points for community gatherings and religious worship. Swahili craftsmen made a living from supplying luxury goods and basic necessities to the towns' residents, learning new skills and techniques from travelling artisans who arrived from across the sea.

The European race for dominance over the spice trade was not long in making its presence felt on the Swahili Coast. In the early 16th century, Vasco da Gama landed on the shores of Mombasa and within a few years the entire coast was under Portuguese dominion. The presence of European invaders brought the golden age of Swahili civilisation to a deadening halt. The great city-states of Kilwa, Mombasa and Zanzibar were sacked and plundered as the Portuguese imposed a tight system of control over Indian Ocean trade, effectively crippling the coast's contacts with the wider world. For almost a century, the mercantile life of the stone towns went into irrevocable decline, never again to recover its former age of wealth and prosperity.

The ruling families of the Swahili Coast fought back, however, and called upon the Mazrui dynasty of Oman to oust the invaders and restore sovereignty to the East African coast. After a series of sieges and battles, Omani Arab fleets ousted the Portuguese from the Swahili Coast and returned to rule in the region. Basing themselves in Zanzibar's Stone Town, the Mazrui dynasty extended their influence as far north as the Lamu Archipelago, governing through a system of ministers and *liwali* well into the 20th century.

The Indian Ocean and its governing trade winds continue to play a large part in Swahili culture. The daily ebb and flow of the tides still govern fishing patterns and sailing routines. The *kusi* and *kaskazi* winds dictate which way annual trade across the Indian Ocean travels during their season. The focal part of any Swahili town is always its port and in the past wooden sailing boats from all over the East African coast and the Indian Ocean moored in larger harbours to sell their cargo, buy goods and rest until the changing winds would carry them home again across the ocean.

The smallest boats, the *mashua* dugout canoe or the small *ngalawa* catamaran, were powered by small *tanga* sails and used by village fishermen for short trips to nearby waters. Larger *dhows* can sail across deep channels and entire oceans with a fairly small crew. The largest of the Swahili trading boats are the grand *jahazi*, their majestic hulls hand-crafted from local mahogany and mangrove wood and built with nothing but the simplest of tools to cross oceans, using only the power of capricious winds.

Right: An incense burner lies within a *zidaka* wall niche at Baytil Ajaib.

The Swahili house is a stately structure, a stone edifice of enduring strength, every corner built to withstand harsh tropical sun and strong monsoons. Stone houses set the residents of Swahili towns apart from their village neighbours, who built their dwellings from mud and wattle, for the sturdy houses were constructed to withstand for centuries the ravages of time. The materials for the houses that line the narrow streets of Swahili stone towns all came from the ocean itself – the beds of old coral quarried for blocks and fired to make lime for mortar and plaster, long mangrove poles cut from sand swamps to line the high ceilings of narrow rooms, reef coral whose soft surfaces made it ideal for carving ornamental lintels and niches.

Wealthy merchant families constructed the oldest houses, their edifices scattered along the waterfronts and ports of the larger Swahili towns. An entire extended family would inhabit the many floors and apartments of the *nyumba* and as generations grew extensions would be added to the family residence. Over time, separate stone houses were built adjacent to the original free-standing structures, and neighbourhoods called *mtaa* gradually developed to create Swahili stone towns as we think of them today – plain facades of high stone buildings, small shuttered balconies and covered latticework windows to protect the womens' modesty, stone *baraza* ledges on the street where local men meet without entering the private space of the merchants' homes.

The inhabitants of the Swahili Coast have long been reverent Muslims and Islamic values played a fundamental part in the division of space and the basic layout of the traditional stone house. Privacy was paramount and stringent customs and norms separated the private from the public sphere. When entering a traditional stone house, no part of the women's quarters or the central courtyard was ever visible from the entrance or the street. Outer windows were heavily shuttered and delicate wooden latticework surrounded most balconies to afford privacy to the women residents who often observed life on the street below. Swahili stone houses also constrcted with air vents and high ceilings to channel ocean winds and keep the area as cool and shaded as possible. The courtyard, rooftop and inner verandas of the house also provided a place for women to enjoy life outdoors without entering the public sphere. Islam prohibits imagery in all art and decoration, so carvers of both wood and plaster worked exclusively with intricate geometric designs, often including patterns flowers, vines and leaves.

Right: An outdoor *baraza* covered with *kikoi* pillows faces sunset at Munira's Camp on Kiwayu Island.

Although their layout, design and decor varied widely depending on their location along the coast, Swahili stone houses shared similar architectural features. Beside traditional *baraza* benches, the *daka* entrance was usually composed of stone steps leading to a carved door, whose geometric designs often indicated the status and origins of the house's owner, whether Arab, Indian or from other ports around the Swahili Coast. Just inside the door but hidden from the public gaze was a staircase that led to the house's upper rooms. On the second floor a small veranda called *msana wa tini* overlooked the *kiwanda* courtyard downstairs. The open air of the *kiwanda* led to common rooms, storerooms, a usually a bathroom, a stairway to the rooftop kitchen and a cistern of fresh well water. It was around the courtyard that much of the daily activities of the household would take place and where the family's livestock and slaves would sleep at night. On the second floor were the private quarters of the house's inhabitants, divided into a series of long horizontal rooms with varying degrees of privacy. The first room set off the *msani wa tini* veranda was commonly used as a bedroom, with both ends screened off by a curtain of expensive fabric hung from a *miwandi* pole built into the wall. The head of the household slept in the most private room of the house, the *ndani*, and an en-suite bathroom and toilet extended to the corner of one side.

Deep in the upstairs rooms, the decorative features of the stone house's rooms increased. Ornamental niches called *zidaka* lined walls and multi-foil arches decorated open doorways that lead to inside rooms. Often, the wall of the master bedroom would have an entire wall of *zidaka* niches, their geometric patterns visible from the outermost room. Carved plaster borders and wall friezes made from coral lime were also a popular feature and often contained a single niche at their centre. Woven rugs covered the soft lime floors but furniture was extremely costly and remained sparse. Hardwood four-poster beds called *pavilao* stood high off the floor, accessible only by use of a small *ntazanyao* stool. Carved wooden chests often decorated with metalwork were used to store clothing and jewellery. Ornate chairs woven with *ute* string were made from hardwood or ebony and used during wedding celebrations and special occasions.

In the small fishing villages that dot the islands and mainland coast, Swahili inhabitants still build their houses in the traditional way, using simple materials and completing regular repairs after seasonal rains. Thin mangrove poles, filled in with hardened mud and large chunks of coral, create the walls of these one-room village dwellings. Thatched palm is woven together to make a *makuti* roof and *mkeka* mats woven from treated palm fronds cover the swept dirt floors. Village houses, usually built in the shade of mango trees and coconut palms, are more exposed to the elements than stone houses built around larger ports.

Throughout the old stone towns and fishing villages of the Swahili Coast there has been a revival of interest in traditional styles, building materials and architecture. UNESCO has recently declared both Stone Town in Zanzibar and the old stone towns of Lamu Island protected World Heritage Sites. Government agencies and residents now endeavour to repair and preserve the stone houses, coral ruins and waterfront edifices that have made the Swahili Coast one of the cultural gems of the African continent.

The properties in this book were selected because they epitomise Swahili style – a conglomeration of traditional architecture and design. Most of them welcome guests and should you be inclined to visit, contact details can be found at the back of the book. It is our hope that in reading about the design styles and architecture of the Swahili Coast, you too will become inspired by its simplicity and sumptuous splendour. *Karibu sana* – welcome and enjoy.

Right: Swahili beds like this one are traditionally inlaid with hand-painted Indian tiles.

Lamu

"At Lamu the sea throws up amber on the shore."

Abu al-Mahasin, 15th century Arab traveller

Just off the coast of northern Kenya lie a profusion of islands that make up the Lamu Archipelago. It was here that the greatest Swahili city-states, feudal networks of rulers and traders governed by the monsoon winds, rose and fell – Siyu, Pate, Shanga and Lamu. Nestled between Manda Island and the vast expanses of the Indian Ocean is Lamu, whose remote location and lasting mystique have made it one of the last untouched outposts of the Swahili Coast, cloaked in tradition and memory, untouched and unchanged by the passage of time.

Although archaeological evidence dates settlement in Lamu to as early as the 9th century, the island only became a thriving city in the 15th century, when Indian Ocean trade bought hundreds of *dhows* from across the ocean to its sheltered bay. In its heyday Lamu was a thriving and cosmopolitan community. Arab and Indian traders married into local society and sailors from around the Indian Ocean brought their knowledge and customs to the port town's bustling streets. As with other prosperous city-states on the East African coast, the arrival of Portuguese invaders in the early 16th century fractured the network of trade alliances that had held the Swahili Coast together for centuries.

With their expulsion at the turn of the 18th century, prosperity again returned to the secluded archipelago but Lamu remained eclipsed by the larger ports of Zanzibar and Mombasa to the south, never again to rise to her former glory. Still, the island's isolation and slip into obscurity saved the archipelago from modernisation and today, the old buildings of Lamu's glory days remain intact and the Swahili way of life still survives in the old town's streets.

Lamu Island is divided into two separate settlements. The old port lies in Lamu Town to the south, where the town's cosmopolitan population of traders, middlemen, sailors and aristocracy built stone houses around the waterfront. A few kilometres to the north lies Shela, a sleepy village of fishermen and small plantations where a few rich merchants built summer houses. Today Shela remains the quieter of the two towns, Lamu still bustling with a vibrant culture of trade and seafaring that made the island into a thriving Indian Ocean port so many centuries ago.

Right: Dhow building along the waterfront between Shela Village and Lamu Town.

Baytil Ajaib

The ultimate Swahili experience

Baytil Ajaib means 'house of wonders' in Arabic and truly this is a magical place. Through its doors opens a private world of light and air, the walls glowing with sunlight, clusters of palms and ferns fanned by the run of breeze through a central courtyard where butterflies and birds flutter and play. Within these walls, the African Arab culture of the Swahili Coast is a tactile and living experience. The house, expertly restored by proprietors Paul Weaver and Norbert Herget, remains exactly as it was built centuries before — totally traditional and Swahili in every way.

Baytil Ajaib is a refuge from the heat and bustle of Lamu Town. A traditional *mdaba* stands before the entranceway and the first floor, which was originally used to store goods and house the merchant family's livestock, has now become a simple yet elegant sitting and dining room. An old well still stands off the courtyard, covered with a large wooden lid, and small fish dart in and out of the light in the cistern nearby. Many of Baytil Ajaib's walls display the shape of a chained turtle in various degrees of abstraction, a Swahili symbol of fertility and prosperity metaphorically bound by religious law and moral restraint. From the rooftop — flat and uncovered in the traditional style — the surrounding houses stretch towards Lamu's port, the sea shimmering in a striking panorama almost unchanged for over a century.

In the late afternoon the whole house glows with sunlight as the breeze chases itself through each room. The upstairs *harem* of the old house has been restored into four interconnecting apartments, airy rooms and open spaces of understated decadence now inhabited by discerning guests. Antique Swahili furniture decorates most of the rooms and what isn't from the pages of history has been painstakingly reproduced from major pieces — an exact replica of the Sultan of Kilwa's bed stands in one of the suites. Niches and alcoves line the walls, some filled with rare antiques of porcelain and brass, copper and silver, some left empty to accentuate the play of light and shadows. The ventilation holes in the walls were crafted in the shape of stars so that incoming light casts dancing patterns of gold across the floor. The rooms are so serene and peaceful, so authentically simple yet completely luxurious, that the entire house seems the stuff of legend and dreams.

Left: Antiques line rows of *zidaka* niches around the entrance to a first floor bedroom. In the traditional Swahili manner, no part of the bedroom — not even the door — is visible from the outside.

Left: From the sheltered entranceway off the main street, the house's courtyard glows gold with direct sunlight.

Right: Geometric shapes adorn the doorway to an inner room, the decorative plasterwork and mangrove poles along the ceiling visible just visible through the archway.

Left: A long mirror reflects the archway of a room off the central courtyard.
Right: Deep red cushions and a striped green *kikoi* on this simple bench create a
deep play of colours.

Left: An exact replica of the Sultan of Kilwa's bed is in one of the bedrooms. Once assembled, the bed is so heavy that it is impossible to move.
Right: A detail of the hardwood carvings on the same bed.

Tusitiri Dhow

Dhow safaris in sultan's style

Across the waters of the Lamu Archipelago, the Tusitiri Dhow makes a majestic first impression. Her white sail furled against the monsoon winds, her mast towering high over the sparkling horizon and her deck shining in the sunlight, the elegant *jahazi* – the largest type of sailing *dhow* on the Indian Ocean – creates an unforgettable silhouette against the African sky. Mark and Richenda Eddy, who sail the *jahazi* around the Lamu Archipelago, have outfitted her in sumptous splendour and Tusitiri embarks on some of the most creative safari expeditions on the Swahili Coast. Safaris last up to a week while guests scuba dive, swim, fish and just generally relax wherever and whenever they desire. For a bit of game viewing from Swahili shores, the *dhow* sails up the hinterland of Dodori Creek on the northern coast of the mainland, where animals can be viewed from the many Indian pillows piled on deck.

Although Tusitiri is furnished in classical Arabian comfort, her design is firmly based in traditional principles of Swahili simplicity. Thick Persian carpets and woven *mkeka* mats cover the hardwood deck, shaded on one side by a canopy of sail cloth. Large pillows of deep blues and reds lie in abundance on deck, perfect for lounging under the tropical sun in between dives and exploring nearby islands. A classic dining room table stands under the mast, where guests linger long after dinner is served to enjoy the stars and watch moon rise. Some nights, sailing is done by the light of the full moon. Bedrolls of light linen and thick mattresses are laid out directly under the stars as the waves of the Indian Ocean gently rock guests to a peaceful sleep.

Despite its adventurous itinerary, the Tusitiri Dhow sails in enough comfort to satisfy even a sultan and his entourage. A wooden shower compartment built against one side of the boat opens to the bright blue sky. In the dressing room below deck, old mirrors with delicately carved wooden borders complement a countertop of elegant blue and white tiles. On deck, gently polished mahogany floors are soft enough for bare feet and glow gently in the sun. Add to this excellent table fare and an completely open itinerary – whether full-on adventure or languorous relaxation – and you have a truly Swahili experience, sailing as the *dhow* merchants did, plying the trade winds under the African sky.

Left: Lunch aboard Tusitiri Dhow is a regal experience, surrounded by natural forests, deserted beaches and quiet waters.

Left: Small lanterns, hardwood chests and bright Indian cushions make the *jahazi's* deck a comfortable place to be.
Right: On board, coffee is served the traditional Swahili way.

Above: A traditional captain's wheel is still used to steer the *jahazi*.
Right (clockwise from top left): A nautical instrument; hand-carved sugar pots; mariners' rope; carved flowers and leaves along the boat's panels.

Kijani House Hotel

Secret gardens and stately Swahili retreats

Off the bustling waterfront of Shela Village, *dhows* sway gently on the incoming tide as merchants and fishermen cross back and forth on the shimmering sand. A few steps away, a small entrance framed by clusters of frangipani and bougainvillaea flowers opens to cool shade and green shadows. Entering Kijani House Hotel is like stepping into a secret garden, an enchanted hotel of private spaces and elegant retreats. Aquamarine pools glow gently in the shade of giant *kunazi* trees, small tables and beach chairs lie under a profusion of palms and flowering flamboyants and yellow oleanders brach out over large terraces that face the ocean. *Kijani* means green in Swahili, at once invoking the colour of Islam, the small hotel's verdant gardens and the fecundity of new growth.

Owner Pierre Oberson and his wife Mwanashee created Kijani to revive the tradition of stone Swahili houses and provide an authentic retreat for visitors looking to experience Lamu's past. It took them more than twenty years to rebuild the hotel from the ruins of three old properties, using only traditional methods and materials in the restoration. Kijani's rooms and gardens are filled with antiques and handmade replicas of the furniture, lanterns, ornaments and utensils that graced the stately houses of Lamu's past. Copies of old Portuguese lamps sway from white archways. An arrangement of ceramic water pots, used to carry oil and water aboard ships centuries ago, stand under the shade of a royal palm. Members of Shela Village even borrow Kijani's antique ceremonial chair, crafted on the nearby island of Siyu, to celebrate weddings and special occasions.

True to the atmosphere of a Swahili home, Kijani's rooms and central areas emphasise the aesthetics of privacy and space. Each room has a private veranda shaded from sight by sculpted archways and trees. The rooms are dark and cool, shards of sunlight and ample breeze welcomed through tall wooden shutters. A canopied Swahili bed stands beside antique cupboards and tables inlaid with hand-coloured Indian tiles and painted glass. In the bathroom, intricately carved mirrors set off the sensuousness of warm ochre walls, the heady oriental effect heightened by shafts of light that filter through the shutters from the world outside. Kijani House Hotel offers a retreat from the bright bustle of Lamu's waterfront – a lush oasis of green gardens, pools and cool rooms in splendid Swahili style.

Left: The entrance off the waterfront secludes Kijani House Hotel from the bustle of Shela Village outside.

Left: A table inlaid with hand-painted Indian tiles and a chair woven with *ute* string look out past a profusion of trees towards the waterfront.

Above: Antique pots used to carry oil and water on long dhow journeys across the Indian Ocean add detail to Kijani's gardens.

Left: Delicate Arab lanterns, a coloured *mkeka* mat and a simple *kikoi* create rich texture in the bedroom.

Right: Ochre-coloured walls, copper pitchers and a woven *mkeka* basket create an opulent atmosphere in the bathroom.

Johari House

A stately Arab villa in the heart of Shela Village

S tepping through the simple carved door at Johari House, a gentle breeze blows gently from the palm fringed entrance. Just beyond lies a sun-filled courtyard, where huge potted ferns and palms sway gently against sand-coloured walls. A small fountain, a traditional feature of stone houses in the Middle East, trickles softly behind a tall pillar, its cool water cascading over colourful Spanish tiles in complex geometric shapes. Just off the courtyard, small *zidaka* niches filled with antique rosewater decanters and Arabian lanterns frame a large wooden door that leads deeper inside. Beyond the old entranceway, a wall displays over a hundred *zidaka* in changing shapes carved into its plaster work – arches and rectangles, squares and arabesques – that reach all the way to the room's high ceiling.

Johari House is a classic Swahili home, its layout simple and understated, its design stately and magnificent. Originally built in the early 19th century by Swahili nobleman Bwana Omari Mokowe for his newlywed daughters, its current owners, Alan and Moira Earnshaw, have changed little of Johari's timeless simplicity. On a wall bordering the courtyard, ornate designs in original plaster work extend around a simple alcove in interwoven patterns of flowers and chains. As in a traditional Swahili home, the deeper you walk into its stone interior, the cooler the rooms become – from the spacious long sitting room to darkened bedrooms cooled by the incoming breeze. The sheer simplicity of Johari's classical Swahili architecture and the profusion of plants and flower motifs transforms it into a garden house, a place of refreshment, seclusion and peace.

Upstairs, Johari House assumes more modern comforts. On the first floor, a large trellis shades an open rooftop garden as bunches of pink bougainvillaea hang from its wooden frame. Ferns in large planters sit beside a whitewashed *baraza* as heavy flowers drop slowly in the gentle breeze. Swahili furniture, all made or sourced locally in Lamu, adorns the the bedrooms in quiet elegance. Coffee braziers and incense burners stand on small tables and the soft sand-coloured floors are piled high with mats and pillows. On the rooftop's large *baraza*, shaded by thatched *mkeka*, lie voluminous cushions in African prints, bright and vibrant against the rooftops of Shela Village and the clear blue sky.

Left: A small bronze ornament stands in the centre of a wall *zidaka* in the sitting room, where a large couch is piled with pillows covered in traditional fabrics.

Above: A frame of various *zidaka* and wall carvings leads to a complex row of geometric *zidaka* in a room downstairs.
Right: Simple furnishings and the play of carvings and colour create a subtle effect that is classic Swahili style.

Peponi Hotel

Classic Swahili elegance in luxurious surroundings

U p and down the Swahili Coast, Peponi Hotel is known for its elegance and bon vivant style. Owned and managed by the Korschen family since 1967, the small hotel is situated on a wide beach in front of Shela Village. Spacious views and hidden corners give the grounds the air of a secluded hideaway. From morning to midnight, *dhows* in full sail ply back and forth from the head of Lamu Channel to the old town, the sailors and fishermen calling greetings to each other over the lapping waves. At Peponi, privacy is paramount. Around the property stand hanging beds shaded by *makuti* thatch and piled with pillows. Private tables and swings stand atop glowing white rooftops shaded by large desert dates and flamboyant trees. Wandering over pathways imprinted with the shapes of large leaves, up winding stairways, and under trellises of flowers, the space is sheltered from the elements yet open and welcoming to the tropical breeze.

The rooms at Peponi are decorated in a graceful mix of contemporary design and Swahili style, with large windows and doors to let in ocean breeze and bright sunlight. Soft muslin curtains, delicately embroidered and so thin as to just filter the light, hang from floor to ceiling. High Swahili beds stand silhouetted behind a gentle canopy of mosquito netting. A bedside vase of pink bougainvillaea contrasts gently with blue and white bedspreads printed in Zimbabwean patterns of geometric fish and geckos, minarets and palm trees. Bathrobes, dressing gowns and beach towels handmade from bright cotton *kikois* add a luxurious Swahili element to swimming in the ocean or the nearby infinity pool sheltered by an ancient baobab.

Peponi Hotel prides itself on small details. *Dhow* eyes hang in an impressive collection on the wall of the central walkway, the Islamic star and crescent moon motif complemented by more unusual designs that include dolphins, a lion and a rhino. In Swahili culture, these carved wooden disks impart boats with symbolic sight and guide the vessel safely through danger. On the shelves of the colonial-style bar, handmade models of wooden *dhows* stand next to nautical maps and sailing implements, pieces collected from life spent near the sea . Original and luxurious, Peponi Hotel balances Swahili style with contemporary comfort and is sure to remain a favourite for many years to come.

Left: The pool reflects the colours of sunset as boats between Lamu Island and Manda Island pass by.

Left: A wall of symmetrical *zidaka* set into the coral and limestone wall add a timeless Swahili elegance to the dining room at Peponi.

Right: A hanging bed shaded with *makuti* thatch and piled with bright pillows overlooks the hotel's infinity pool.

Left: Folded frangipani flowers transform a stone footbath into a luxurious experience.

Right: A rich tropical garden lush with indigenous plants and colourful flowers accentuates the angles and arches of the hotels' rooms.

Shela and Palm House

Spacious villas in sophisticated style

Shela and Palm House lie on the back streets of Shela Village not far from the waterfront bustling with *dhows* and donkeys. As with all traditional Swahili houses, the outside is sparse and minimal, with shuttered windows and a white exterior built high against the tropical sun. Once you enter through the houses' carved wooden doors, though, a private world emerges. Open courtyards shaded green with potted palms and ferns lead to sheltered stairways and interior verandas, spacious sitting areas and arched windows that bespeak simple comforts and timeless elegance. Although Shela and Palm House are two separate and distinct properties, the two villas stand side by side and can be singled out from the other stone houses of Shela Village by the shock of flowering vines that grow on the buildings' exteriors and drop magenta petals gracefully onto the open street.

Shela House was converted to a villa by one of the first European settlers in Lamu, who constructed it over the ruins of a previous stone house near the site of an old village well. Just inside the entrance stands the frame of an old *ngalawa* boat. Navigational maps hang on the walls near woven *mkeka* sun hats in case guests feel like a stroll along the waterfront. The house itself is airy and spacious, full of warm light that streams through the windows and the verdant courtyard where yellow oleander trees and a profusion of climbing vines set the soft white walls ablaze with colour. The dining room and *baraza*-style sitting room both open to the courtyard, as do most rooms in the villa. Four-poster Swahili beds and hand-carved local furniture give the bedrooms and sitting rooms upstairs a timeless feel.

Palm House is named after the single royal palm that graces the entrance to the villa, decorated in sophisticated yet simple African coastal style. Like Shela House, the central courtyard is a focal point of life in the villa and the play of colours on the golden floors and white walls comes to life in the evening light. The downstairs rooms are decorated with printed textiles from Zimbabwe and oil paintings by Gabriela Trzebinski decorate the walls. Bright geometric prints from around Africa cover the bedrooms and communal areas of the property. From both rooftops, the minaret of the Friday Mosque is clearly visible, the ocean peaking in between the palms and rooftop gardens of Shela Village.

Left: Wooden latticework above the archways lets patches of light into the dining room at Palm House.

Left: Gentle archways lead to the *baraza*-style sitting room at Shela House.
Right (clockwise from top left): The dark wood of a dining table brings out the shutters on a window facing outside at Shela House; Shela House's *baraza* pillows and a Persian rug bring bright colour to the interior; an engraved copper plate, coloured window and simple chair create a typical Arabian-inspired scene at Shela House; the play of colours of the stairway, walls and fern complement each other at Shela House

Left: Relaxing on a hammock on the roof of Shela House is the perfect place to watch life unfold around Shela Village and the waterfront.
Right: Paintings by Gabriela Trzebinski add a sophisticated element to the sitting room at Palm House.

Moon Houses

Stately Swahili villas in oriental style

Off the quiet streets of Shela Village, not far from waterfront of Lamu Bay, stand two houses separated by a tranquil pool. For architect and designer Bernard and Anita Spoerry, Kiwandani and Full Moon House are the culmination of a vision that has encompassed more than two decades of building and decorative work. Built in the spirit of traditional Lamu architecture, the two houses are a joint creation where the art of oriental living is a contemporary reality. Full Moon, a Swahili villa with four balcony-filled floors that face out to the waterfront, and Kiwandani, with its spiralling passageways and secret *baraza*, combine eastern tastes with modern comfort.

Both houses are built with natural materials in neutral earth tones in keeping with Lamu's unique version of Swahili style. Heavy shutters of dark wood open against walls of white limestone and chalk coral, small shapes carved out of the heavy frames to splay bright crosses and stars across the cool floors. Pots of papyrus and ferns frame spiralling staircases that lead to sparkling white terraces eye-level with the tops of palm trees. Both master bedrooms are private kingdoms with secluded roof gardens and spacious *baraza* from which to watch the changing tides. In Kiwandani, a three-tiered chandelier made of Venetian, Moroccan and Turkish glass in a myriad of shapes and sizes scatters magical light in the master bedroom's private sitting room. The two houses are joined by a long pool, its pale water shimmering in the shade of towering frangipani and palm trees. A long *baraza* piled high with giant pillows stretches against the wall to provide a shaded corridor beside the thick green grass, its sandstone coloured walkway glowing deeply in the afternoon sun.

Choosing the furniture, colour schemes and opulent textiles that adorn both Moon Houses was Anita's job and she scoured the markets and bazaars of India, East Africa and the Middle East in search of each individual piece that now adorns the properties' niches and walls, small alcoves and passageways. Bernard has a dedicated passion for the revival of Swahili architecture in the Lamu style and his activism, studies and numerous publications have gone a long way towards promoting the conservation of Lamu Island's old houses and buildings. For both of them, the Moon Houses are a continued passion – beautiful treasures that allow guests to experience the lavish wonder of Swahili life.

Left: The sitting room at Full Moon House is decorated in authentic Swahili style, with antique dishes inset in the *zidaka*, Persian rugs and a traditional wedding chair.

Left: A traditional Siyu door leads to the the master bedroom of Kiwandani House. The covered *baraza* and rest of the balcony is ideal for watching the waterfront and rooftop of Shela Village.

Right: Bright *baraza* and day beds lie in the shaded passageway beside the swimming pool that connects Full Moon to Kiwandani House.

Above: Venetian, Moroccan and Turkish glass make up the colourful chandelier in Kiwandani House's master bedroom. Large *zidaka*, dark shutters and a low table inlaid with hand-painted Indian tiles adds to the Swahili atmosphere.
Right: An antique Swahili wedding chair, dark wood furniture and a high bed create a stately atmosphere in this bedroom at Kiwandani House.

Beach House

A classic modernist villa built for the trade winds

At the northern end of Shela Village, just off the pebbled sands of Lamu Bay, stands Beach House – a majestic tribute to a fusion of Mediterranean modernism and Swahili style. Neutral colours and wide, airy rooms create a living environment that is open and at one with the natural beauty of Lamu. The house is cloaked in brilliant white, the better to accentuate the shadows of the tropical sun and delicate branches of the many indigenous trees growing tall in the terraced gardens. Old acacias reach up to the rooftop terrace, where the dazzling white floor and arabesque balustrades seem to pierce open the sky.

It is the notion of space in Beach House that makes the property so elegant and superbly stylish. Each of the sun-filled bedrooms are swathed in embroidered Indian cloth and gauzy curtains flutter gracefully to reveal patches of azure ocean and the tips of acacia and baobab trees outside. In the dazzling light of the late afternoon, the terraces glow with golden light, their brilliant white setting off the shifting colours of the darkening water and sky. Large shuttered windows open to bougainvillaea filled gardens carefully nurtured from the banks of a reclaimed sand dune, where tropical birds twitter and play from dawn to dusk. Communal space is expansive and comfortable, with large piles of pillows covered in Zimbabwean *kuba* cloth in the central sitting room and African artefacts and art carefully displayed in minimalist style in the many corners and archways.

Beach House was designed with the changing monsoon winds in mind and each of the house's open terraces offers shelter and protection against one of the seasonal winds. It is this perceptible link with the changing rhythms of Swahili life that makes the property feel so at one with its environment. The entrance from the waterfront is an old Swahili door, behind which small steps, covered by a trellis of flowering vines, make their way up the hillside to the villa. On the ground floor, an aquamarine infinity pool appears just level with the gentle waters of Lamu Bay as stately columns of chiselled white rise on either side of the house to produce clean, modernist angles. The classic simplicity of Beach House is an elegant statement in Swahili style, a dedicated minimalism that complements and enhances its environment.

Left: The entrance to Beach House opens to classic pillars and an inviting infinity pool.

Left: A *baraza* on the rooftop terrace overlooks Lamu Bay and Manda Island.
Right: Carvings on a Swahili chair bring out the subtle colours of the wood.

Kipungani Explorer

Romantic beach hideaways between sand dunes and the sea

Located on a remote beach on Lamu Island, Kipungani Explorer offers unparalleled relaxation in isolated and completely natural surroundings. After a short boat journey from Lamu Town, the thatched roofs of the lodge emerge surrounded on all sides by palm trees and sparkling water. Sand dunes crowned with scrub bush and palm trees tower high in the distance and across the water lies Manda Island, a thick forest of mangrove trees and swooping storks. At dawn, the rising sun transforms the ocean into patches of shining silver as sandbars at low tide stretch out into the water like golden fingers. From early morning to sunset, the only sounds are the soft lapping of the waves, the rustling of palm trees and the calls of birds making their way across the islands. As silent *dhows* drift from horizon to horizon over still waters, the noises and bustle of civilisation feel far, far away.

Between the shimmering water and the golden dunes, fourteen beach huts open out to the ocean. Made from all-natural materials, the *banda* cottages – some built high on wooden stilts, others just metres from the water – stand completely open to the beach, shaded on either side by bamboo blinds that seclude the other rooms from sight. Large clam shells hold water for a sand-rinsing foot bath. On the veranda, a hanging bed piled with pillows swings gently back and forth in the ocean breeze. Inside, a four-poster bed stands shaded by a billowing mosquito net and behind a woven *mkeka* screen lies a private dressing room, bathroom and solar-heated shower.

Everything at Kipungani is built with natural luxury in mind. The dining area and bar are decorated with gnarled branches of driftwood smoothed by the passage of time. On a balcony built high on stilts over the water, hanging beds in the shade of a *makuti* roof stand out in bright patterns against the dark wood and *mkeka* mats that cover the floors and furniture. Beachcombers' treasures abound. Pale-coloured shells rest in glass bowls, driftwood branches lean against the corners and large clam shells found around the island are scattered along sand pathways in abundant profusion. Kipungani's remote location and eco-friendly approach make it a perfect hideaway for romantics and castaways who want none of the trappings of the civilised world, but all its comforts.

Left: On the veranda, a hanging bed shaded by *makuti* thatch faces out towards the beach.

Left: Made from all natural materials, the rooms at Kipungani feel free and close to nature.

Right: Bungalows thatched with *makuti* make for spacious rooms and lookout points at Kipungani Explorer.

Munira's Camp

Kiwayu Island, all to yourself

Perched high on a sandy ridge surrounded by ocean and wilderness, Munira's Camp is just about as far from the civilised world as you're likely to get. The only property on Kiwayu Island, the camp's design is simple yet supremely comfortable and enchanting. For sheer remoteness and untouched beauty, Munira's Camp is unmatched. The island's beach, a short walk through sand dunes and sheltering acacias, stretches as far as the eye can see. Low scrub and wild bush cover sand dunes that rise like guardians from the white-capped surf and what's more, you can be indulgently selfish, for there's not another person in sight.

Owner Mike Kennedy has lived in the Lamu Archipelago for twenty years and knows the area and its islands intimately. To the west, Dodori Game Reserve and Boni Forest Reserve extend to the horizon and the small islands and mangrove channels between Kiwayu and the mainland are covered in unadulterated green. The island stretches fourteen kilometres from north to south but is only five hundred metres wide, which means that both the archipelago's islands and the open sea are visible from most of the seven bungalows. The waters on either side of the island lie within Kiungo Marine National Reserve, a protected area that extends all the way to the Somali border sixty kilometres to the north. The vibrant reef formations, breathtaking coral and hordes of tropical fish are made all the more spectacular because you are absolutely the only one there.

The sheer beauty that surrounds Munira's Camp means that decoration is best kept to a minimum. Each of the *banda* cottages are perched high on island's ridge and placed at distant intervals to provide maximum privacy and space. All made of natural materials, *mkeka* and *makuti*, they have been designed to make little impact on the surrounding bush and indeed blend seamlessly into the natural environment. Fresh water for showers is carried up from the island's well by hand and both the shower and bathroom look out in total privacy towards mangrove channels and islands or empty stretches of virgin beach. Three sides of each *banda* open to wilderness and the sea, beside piled with pillows and soft hammocks perfect for gazing towards the pristine horizon. Shells and driftwood, oil paintings of sea creatures, and blue and white *kanga* bed and pillow covers create an easy atmosphere of comfort in total harmony with nature.

Left: A hanging bed looks west towards sunset over mangrove creeks and the Dodori Game Reserve.

Left: Simple rooms left open to the natural environment and made from local materials make each bungalow a superb balance between easy comfort and the exquisiteness of nature.

Right: Hammocks and chairs border vast windows overlooking the narrow expanse of Kiwayu Island.

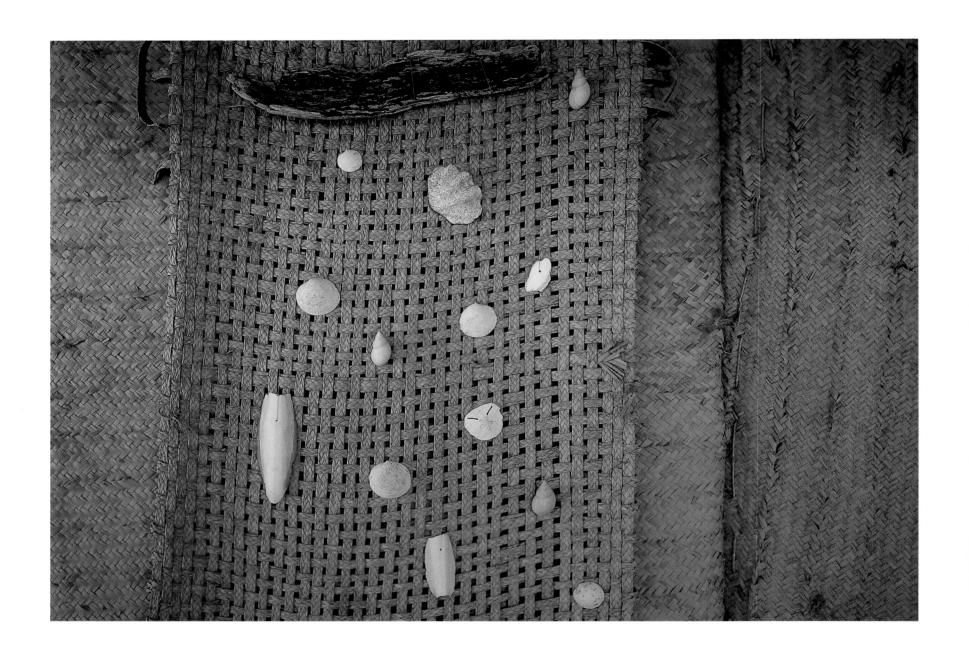

Left: Sand-dollars, driftwood, cuttlefish bones and shells adorn the *mkeka* covered doors of one of the bungalows.

Right (clockwise from top left): A green glass buoy borders a bungalow doorway; beaded shells hang before the hallway entrance; woven *mkeka* even covers the shelves; plenty of open space makes the rooms truly spectacular.

Left: A brilliant blue painting of a sea turtle contrasts against the simple tan of woven *mkeka* walls.

Right: The wide beach on the east side of Kiwayu Island is magical, untouched and expansive.

Oils and Incense

"Within me is the fire of hell, but without floats the perfume of paradise."
Anonymous engraving, 18th century Persian incense burner

For a thousand years, fragrance has played an important part in life on the Swahili Coast. With the arrival of ships from Arabia and India in the 9th and 10th centuries, the use of incense and perfume was rapidly incorporated into the traditions and rituals of the East African coast. What developed was a blend of magic and religion, ornament and superstition that survives to this day. On the shelf of every good *duka* shop stands a glass bowl filled with incense to ward off the many kinds of *sheitani* and *jinn* that meddle in the daily affairs of mere mortals. No Swahili home would be complete without cones of incense resting near the *jiko*, or charcoal brazier.

Incense and perfume oils played an essential part in Indian Ocean trade and were a valuable commodity from the times of the ancients. Myrrh, a traditional stimulant, continues to grow on the punishing rocks of the Somali coast. The best frankincense trees, known for their healing properties, can still be found in the deserts of Oman. Plantations of sandalwood thrive in southern India and their oil, reputed to contain aphrodisiac properties, remains a common ingredient in incense and perfumes. To make incense, powdered resin or perfume oils are mixed – often in secret quantities – with sandalwood bark to make a thick paste. Once dried, the burning paste emits a trail of smoke that slowly permeates the room with striking scents.

Apart from their pleasing fragrances, incense and perfume oils have also held a time-honoured place in traditional beliefs along the Swahili Coast. Like their Arab and Indian counterparts across the ocean, coastal people believe in a complex spirit world. Called *arit*, *jinn* or *sheitani*, these capricious spirits inhabit an invisible but parallel world and can live for over three hundred years. They love to interfere and meddle in human activities and are held responsible for a myriad of misfortunes, from bad luck to madness. Special combinations of incense and scented oils ward off the spirits since, according to a shopkeeper in Lamu, "*Jinn* despise anything that smells pleasant." So it is that in the bazaars and houses of the Swahili Coast, the odours of myrrh, frankincense and sandalwood hang heavy on the evening air, seeping the streets with the scents of the orient.

Left: Incense burners come in a variety of shapes and sizes.
Right: Covered with a *kanga* cloth, this incense burner is used for perfuming women's hair and clothes.

Mombasa

"On Saturday we cast anchor off Mombasa. No sooner had we been perceived than a small boat manned by Moors came out to us. In front of the city there lay numerous vessels all dressed in flags."

Vasco Da Gama, 1498

The buildings and gardens in the old city of Mombasa tell of a legacy of conquest and battle for control over the trade ways and caravan routes that led from the hinterland of the African continent to Arabia, India and beyond. Although old city was first mentioned by the Arab traveller Al Idrisi in 1154, the area's prosperity peaked in the 15th century when it competed with Swahili city-states including Kilwa Kisiwani to the south for dominance over Indian Ocean trade. These days, Mombasa remains the major port of the Kenyan coast, although the wind-filled *dhows* and old custom houses that made the city famous for centuries remain a thing of the past.

Portuguese explorer Vasco de Gama was the first European to arrive in Mombasa in 1498, looking to expand his country's trade routes and bring Christian influence to the East African coast. The town heroically resisted invasion and the Portuguese moved to Malindi further north to establish a permanent settlement. For the next hundred years, the European invaders besieged and burned Mombasa on four separate occasions and in 1589 Mombasa finally succumbed to Portuguese control. Today, the ruins of Fort Jesus remain the most visible signs of the invaders' presence, its ochre-stained walls a tribute to the men who fought and died for a Swahili trading town so far from home.

The old town of Mombasa remains a living testament to the prosperity which made this part of the coast a centre of Swahili civilisation. By the middle of the 19th century, the entire area was under the control of Omani Arabs governing from Zanzibar and remained under the Sultanate's control until the Zanzibar Revolution in 1963. In the neighbourhoods of the old town, the architecture remains a blend of styles, from traditional Swahili houses inspired by the stone houses of Lamu to British colonial and Indian influences that travelled north from Zanzibar. Although much smaller in size than Zanzibar's Stone Town or Lamu Town to the north, the old town of Mombasa remains an important Swahili centre in its own right, its gates, mosques, custom house and old markets a tribute to the importance of travel and trade on the East African coast.

Left: Solitary *dhows* pass the waterfront as the ocean reflects the evening light.

Serena Beach Hotel

A large beach hotel with classic Swahili features

The Serena Beach Hotel is something truly special – a large hotel that has all the elegance and style of a small designer property. Through the hotel's gates a lavish garden of towering palms and thick grass, small *baraza* benches and trellised vines is set back to offer privacy and shade. A domed tower, built in the style of traditional Swahili minarets, interrupts the canopy of palm trees with its brilliant white facade. Throughout the winding gardens, tall frangipani trees drop their gently scented blossoms to lay a carpet of cream and butter coloured flowers. Along the beach front, the haven of green abruptly gives way to fine white sand which at low tide leads to small pools full of starfish and hermit crabs, perfect for hours of exploring.

The main entrance of the Serena Beach Hotel is built in a style reminiscent of Swahili trading *dhows*. The long reception room is full of traditional Swahili decor. Straight-backed wicker chairs inlaid with bone and made from local hardwood face a row of arched *zidaka* niches where each of the room keys are kept. The long hall leads to a piqued archway inset with the painted porcelain serving dishes that arrived on the East African coast from Holland, India and as far away as China and Japan. Planters' chairs line the sitting room and leads to a courtyard where hotel's main meals are served. At night, the entrance to the reception room is lit with soft glowing lanterns and from the outside, framed by fan palms, the hotel shimmers with stately and inviting elegance.

It's the little details at the Serena Beach Hotel that make the property so unique among the large hotels of Mombasa. Throughout the grounds, authentic Swahili furnishings and antiques add a special touch to the graceful buildings. The archway at the end of the reception room leads to an open courtyard where an ornamental pond stretches towards the swimming pool and the ocean. The upstairs terrace bar, where an old Swahili *mzee* plays Beethoven and light jazz as the sun goes down, opens to treetops and the ocean breeze. Antique ceremonial horns called *siwa*, Swahili chests, and an impressive collection of traditional jewellery displayed throughout the property make Serena Beach Hotel a large hotel with definitive style, classically Swahili.

Left: The classic architecture of the Mombasa Serena's main area can be seen in its courtyard, angled walls and colonial style verandas.

Left: The long reception room, its ceiling and furnishings traditionally Swahili, is an authentic example of classical style.

Right: High-backed Swahili chairs and carved tables complement the archways and columns of the Mombasa Serena's reception room.

Alfajiri Villas
Beach side villas in African chic

Stepping into Alfajiri, you are greeted with the sight of water. A goldfish pond studded with stepping stones leads to an open area overlooking an infinity pool that merges indelibly with the crashing waves of the ocean. Alfajiri Villas comprises three separate houses, each one decorated to perfection in a unique style. The Clifftop Villa stands high on a hill overlooking the surf, its infinity pool cut against a backdrop of water and sky, the rooms designed in an elegant combinatoin of Mediterranean and Swahili style. On the opposite end of the property, the Beach Villa is a cosmopolitan showcase of contemporary African style that looks out to the waterfront. In between the two, the Garden Villa faces lightly scented frangipani trees and blossoming desert rose before openning to the beach. The last two houses are recent additions to a remarkable property that continues to lead the way in designer chic on the Kenyan coast.

The Beach Villa comprises long colonial-style verandas with rooms filled with artefacts and unique pieces that blend Swahili style and contemporary African chic. Floor-to-ceiling curtains in West African prints of bold geometric shapes and thick cream-coloured *marekani* hang before large shuttered doors that form the sides of every room. Warm sand-coloured walls and floors glow in the light of handmade lamps, whose silhouettes create strong outlines against the billowing fabrics. Antique planters' chairs and large sofas line the veranda, the villa walls edged with desert rose and frangipani trees. All around the Beach Villa and Alfajiri's main area, the balcony railing, wall dividers and *makuti* roof partitions have used long poles to create the shape of a sun with extended rays, a reminder that in Swahili the property's name means 'dawn.'

As unique as Alfajiri's individual rooms are, it is the villas' central area that brings the property together as a stylistic whole. West African textiles and geometric designs blend with traditional furnishings to create a superbly elegant pan-African theme. A long *baraza* and magnificent sofas piled with zebra-striped pillows frame an aquamarine infinity pool that extends towards the horizon. Stately wooden coffee tables edged in a geometric motif hold antique Omani daggers beneath their glass tops. Palm wigs hang below hand-carved wooden panels that decorate each wall and a driftwood statue by Armando Tanzini – a modern take on an ancient Egyptian goddess – faces longingly towards the ocean.

Left: Bold zebra prints and artefacts from around the continent create an African atmosphere in the main area of Alfajiri Villas.

Left: The entrance to Alfajiri Villas is bold in its use of African antiques, creative materials and the continent's inspiration.

Right (clockwise from top left): African geometric details carved in relief; an elegant lamp silhouette; a carving of an Indian elephant becomes a sophisticated art deco lamp; strong geometric patterns carved into the border of a tabletop form the backbone of a room's design.

Left: Bold Zimbabwean cloth covers a sumptuous couch in the Beach Villa, a large bowl and carved table adding to the African ambiance.

Right: The dining area of Alfajiri a combination of styles from around the African continent, from the Moroccan henna painted lamp to a Masai beaded table runner and copper urn filled with frangipani flowers.

Funzi Keys

Private island on the edge of a marine park

South of Mombasa town, on the edge of Kisite Marine Park, a patchwork of forested islands hides Funzi Keys from view. This privately-owned island is a haven of secluded privacy and natural style, where sweeping views of the keys, sandbars and marine park create splendid vistas of ocean and green. Owned by Alessandro Torriani and his wife Claudia, Funzi Keys is a tribute to the nature that surrounds it. Themes of water and verdure are dominant motifs throughout the property, a tribute to the rich life and lush vegetation that envelops the area, both under the water and above it.

The Funzi Keys' main area is thatched with an impressive makuti roof and stands completely open to the ocean breeze. The structure is built around a towering mangrove tree, its timeworn trunk smooth with age. Downstairs, a retired *dhow* stands majestically in the corner, its deck strewn with antiques and Swahili artefacts that tell of mariners' lives on the East African coast. Globe-shaped glass buoys, their colours a melange of green and blue, lie on deck next to a weathered Omani dagger and traditional brass coffee set. The resident parrot, who has mastered local bird calls, perches near the old *dhow*, giving the main area the colourful and lively atmosphere of a pirate's deck. Traditional roofs laid with fossilised coral and long wooden poles evoke the natural feel of a traditional Swahili home. Around each open archway that faces the beach, local *fundi* workmen have chiselled arabesque designs of flowing lines and flower petals elaborately by hand.

Each room at Funzi Keys lies on a secluded patch of the small island, which stretches more than a kilometre in length but in some places is only thirty metres wide. Perched just on the edge of the beach, shaded by tall pine trees and indigenous mangroves, the rooms are spacious and completely open to the tropical elements. Private sun chairs face out to the water and an area for midnight bonfires transforms each bungalow into relaxing haven in its own right. Four-poster carved beds, antique Swahili chests and a *ngalawa* boat converted into a splendid coffee table add character to the generously sized rooms. In each bungalow, a private jacuzzi looks out towards waves lapping gently on the sands just metres away, the beach made totally private for the utmost in castaway luxury.

Left: A full moon illuminates a table set for a romantic dinner on the beach, the dramatic *makuti* structure of the main area visible in the background.

Left: Brilliantly coloured sofas, the trunk of an old mangrove tree and a sailing *dhow* decorate the sitting room at Funzi Keys.

Right: The carvings and *dhow* eye on the prow of the wooden sailing boat are traditional boat features along the Swahili Coast.

Left: A small *ngalawa* sailing boat makes a creative coffee table in one of the rooms.
Right: Bright pillows and a converted *ngalawa* create a harmonious atmosphere in the spacious rooms.

Kangas, Kitenges and Kikois

"Kikulacho ki nguoni mwako."
That which eats you up is in your clothing.
Kanga proverb

I n the markets and main streets of Swahili towns and villages, textiles in bright and brilliant colours hang on display under the tropical sun. Cloth of all kind is on sale, from sets of printed *kangas* and heavy bolts of *kitenges* to softly woven *kikois* fluttering gently in the breeze. Although most women's tailored clothes are made from *kitenges*, a thick cloth printed with traditional patterns and sold by the metre, pairs of *kanga* cloth remain women's fabric of choice throughout East Africa.

Kangas are probably the most popular, versatile and easily recognisable fabric worn along the Swahili Coast. Worn only by women, *kangas* are a length of cotton cloth that measures long enough to stretch from waist to ankle and wrap securely around the body. *Kangas* were originally invented along the Swahili Coast about a century ago – divergent accounts cite both Mombasa and Zanzibar as their birthplace – when women began sewing bandanas or kerchiefs called *leso* together to create a colourful and multipurpose wrap. Named after the mottled feathers of the *kanga* bird, or guinea fowl, local merchants soon began manufacturing and selling them in a variety of designs. Although *kanga* styles have become increasingly more sophisticated over the years, most of their classic features have remained the same. They are still sold in matching pairs and used for everything from veils and skirts to baby slings and cleaning rags. Geometric patterns and floral motifs are still the most popular designs and an important element of the *kanga* remains the Swahili proverb positioned on the bottom centre of each piece.

The men of the Swahili Coast traditionally wear *kikois* under their white *kanzu* robes. Originally hand-woven in the coastal villages of Somalia, *kikois* are made of soft cotton and their threads run in horizontal stripes in different colours from fringe to fringe. Paired with an over shirt, leather sandals and a Siyu knife, this mainstay of men's clothing is recognisable by its band of thickly woven cloth, or *tirazi*, at either end and a woven fringe of hand-twisted strings, called *matavuwe*. These days *kangas*, *kitenges* and *kikois* are still worn by the women and men of the Swahili Coast, their vivid colours complementing the bright blue of the Indian Ocean and the vibrant green of the palm trees swaying overhead.

Left: Bright, bold designs of traditional kanga.
Right: Traditional Kitenge fabric.

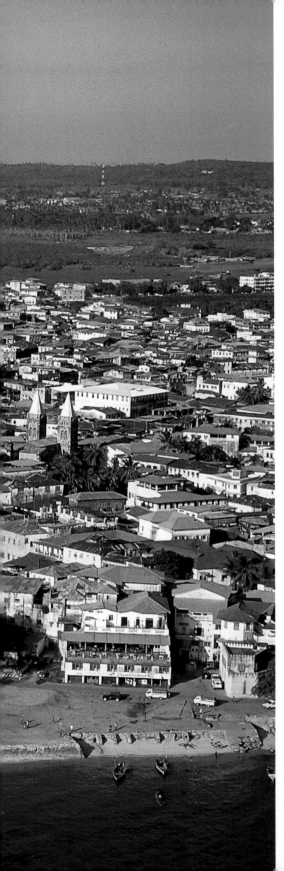

Zanzibar

"As the stranger passes close to the deeply verdant shores of Zanzibar Island, he views nature robed in the greenest verdure, with a delightful freshness of leaf, exhaling fragrance to the incoming wanderer."

Henry Stanley, *Through the Dark Continent*

Whisper the name Zanzibar and immediately visions of passing *dhows* laden with spices and ivory, opulent sultans in coral-hewn palaces and black-robed women wandering through narrow streets are conjured up, proof of the island's lasting enchantment. In Arabic it is called Zinj ib-Bar, or 'land of the blacks,' a term that alluded to the island's importance in the slave trade. Around 700 B.C., the Greek travelogue *Periplus of the Erythraean Sea* refers to Arab trading towns in the area, but it was only with the rise of the city-states and Indian Ocean trade in the 10th century that Zanzibar became a focal point for export and trade, one of the gems of Swahili civilisation on the East African coast.

Today the port city of Stone Town is the largest inhabited Swahili settlement still in existence along the East African coast. Like other Swahili city-states, Zanzibar's prosperity peaked between the 12th and 15th century, before Portuguese invaders arrived to dismantle local merchants' trade routes and control Indian Ocean commerce. The Omani Arabs, who drove the Portuguese invaders out in the late 16th century, than took control of the entire Swahili Coast and chose Zanzibar as their seat of government. Under their influence, the island's return to prosperity was so great that at one point, the Masrui dynasty of Oman moved court to Zanzibar, building vast coral palaces and the stately House of Wonders along the waterfront.

With the total British ban on the slave trade in 1873, Zanzibar's economic importance was suddenly curtailed, the human cargo that had made it rich no longer a viable export. Although spices, ivory and ambergris continued to be an important source of income, the island's golden age was never to return. In 1862, Zanzibar capitulated to the rising influence of Empire in the region and became a British protectorate, retaining its independence only in name. A century later, a violent revolution seized majority control from the sultan's hands, ending the days of dynasty and palace intrigue on the islands of the archipelago. Although the streets of Stone Town remain much as they did centuries ago, the sultans' palaces and retreats slowly give way to time and surrender to the sun and sea.

Left: The old buidlings, winding streets and watefront of Stone Town create an enticing panorama from the air.

Zanzibar Serena Inn

An oasis in the heart of Stone Town

Wander the narrow alleyways of Stone Town towards the waterfront out of its labyrinthine streets and a small square garlanded with frangipani and flamboyant trees emerges. Beneath the shade of a century-old tamarind, a whitewashed bench faces the entrance to the Zanzibar Serena Inn. Gentle steps lead to an oasis of calm in the midst of the old town's stone houses, apartments and palaces. Doormen dressed in long *kanzu* robes and Turkish fez stand beside a stately carved door which opens to a veritable oasis. As you enter the Serena Zanzibar Inn, the ever-present bustle of commerce and local news traded through the winding passageways of the old town fades to the soothing sound of water and wind.

Two Stone Town landmarks straddle the site of the small hotel, the old Extelecoms Building and the Chinese doctor's residence, and both had to be intensely restored in the creation of the Zanzibar Serena. The colonial-style Extelecoms Building was constructed by the British in the early 20th century and served as a hub for the Empire's underwater telegraphic cable network, which at the time encircled the entire globe. The Chinese doctor's residence was actually an old Arab house whose foundation predates much of old Stone Town. In the 1940's and 1950's, it became the residence of the British Consul and in the late 1990's, the Aga Khan Trust for Culture restored both buildings, bringing craftsmen from India, Kenya and mainland Tanzania in an effort to rehabilitate the property and transform it into a luxury hotel.

The Zanzibar Serena Inn was decorated in traditional Zanzibar style, a blend of Omani Arab, Indian and British Victorian influences that translated the interiors and furnishings of the two old buildings into a peaceful urban retreat. Old black-and-white photographs of the House of Wonders and Forodhani Gardens line the walls of the public areas. A few antique brass instruments — some dating back to the 18th century — are all that remain of the old Extelecoms Building, and hang framed behind the bar next to a collection of the 18th century Dutch plates so prized by wealthy Swahili families a century ago. The Zanzibar Serena Inn retains the feel of an old stone house on the waterfront — tiled fountains gurgle gently in the reception area, chandeliers hang above antique wooden furniture and frangipani flowers drop onto balconies perched elegantly above the crashing waves.

Left: The sophisticated rooms at the Zanzibar Serena are a blend of colonial and Swahili Arab style.

Left: Spiced coffee served in the traditional Swahili way is an important ritual at the Zanzibar Serena Inn.

Right: Antique plates from Europe and China, prized by the sultan and his aristocracy, adorn the walls of the hotel. Traditional pots and furniture add a classic Swahili element to the decor.

Left: An open window lets in gentle light to the *baraza*-style sitting room. An antique porcelain plate stands on the carved wooden table.

Right: Stained-glass windows add an exotic element to the Zanzibar Serena Inn's already lavish rooms.

Emerson & Green

Arabian splendour in Zanzibar's old town

No other property on the island captures the essence of Zanzibar like Emerson & Green. This small hotel in the backstreets of Stone Town invokes the island's history and culture with an authenticity and passionate flair that is second to none. Named after the long-time residents who created the hotel over a decade ago, the original structure dates from the late 19th century and belonged to Sir Tharia Topan, the eminent Zanzibari who also built the Old Dispensary. The hotel itself is considered a showpiece of Zanzibar design and décor, its rooms and passageways filled with centuries-old antiques where the art of Swahili living truly comes alive.

In keeping with the hotel's unique style and charm, each of its ten rooms has been designed and decorated in their own character and style. On the third-floor rooftop, the East, West and North rooms are the oldest in the hotel and afford expansive views of Stone Town in classic Zanzibar style. Antique four-poster beds hung with gauzy netting are the centrepieces of each room, with deep colours, stained glass windows and carved wooden doors adding to the *Arabian Nights* atmosphere. The rooms on the lower levels are just as magnificent, from the spacious grandeur of the Ballroom to the chic elegance of the Zenana. Bathtubs in each room recreate something of the opulence of an *Arabian hammam* and lie on balconies sheltered under flowering trellises or sunken into a floor surrounded by antique tiles.

The ultimate Emerson & Green experience is indubitably dinner at the Towertop Restaurant, which has become something of an institution in Zanzibar. The rooftop of the hotel is one of the highest points in Stone Town, second only to the House of Wonders, and affords a breathtaking view of the old city, from Forodhani Gardens and the waterfront to Shangani's melange of stone houses and minarets. Come sunset, guests assemble for drinks at the parapet, savouring a bird's eye view of passing *dhows*. After a three-course meal of Swahili specialities flavoured with the best local spices, guests relax to live music and spiced *kahawa* as the stars shine over Stone Town. Downstairs, a coffee shop named for *taraab* singer Bi Kidude memorializes the life and music of this legendary local diva. From romantic rooftop dining to splendid Swahili quarters, Emerson & Green remains the ultimate in Zanzibar chic.

Left: Soft light creates an immediately oriental atmosphere at the reception room of the small hotel.

Left: One of the hotel's most famous rooms, the Ballroom is decorated in blue tones that complement the black and white tiles on the checkered floor.
Right: A collection of antiques from around the the archipelago makes each room a unique collaboration of history and designer chic.

Left: The legendary rooftop of Emerson & Green affords sweeping views of all of Stone Town and is a perfect place for an evening sundowner or romantic rooftop meal.

Right: This carved Swahili door leads to one of the most famous rooftop rooms, its entranceway decorated with hibiscus, ferns and a sweeping staircase.

Jafferji's House

An Indian townhouse in the heart of Stone Town

Contact between the Indian subcontinent and the East African coast has long played a central part in the development of Swahili style. In Zanzibar especially, the influence of Indian merchant families who for centuries have kept strong ties to the island is easily visible, from the shuttered fronts of long-established shops to rooftop tearooms high above Stone Town's winding streets. Although Indian merchants and sailors had long traded in Zanzibar's thriving port, permanent large-scale settlement on the island only occurred in the 19th century, around the time Hassan Bhai Jafferji bought the house that would become his family home, filling it with antiques and special memories that still flourish four generations later.

The Shangani area, in which the Jafferji House is located, is the oldest and most architecturally intriguing part of Zanzibar's old city. True to the Indian style of the island's community, the house adheres to an elegant combination of elaborate finishing and time-tested Swahili design. A deep *baraza* set off the bustling commercial thoroughfare of Gizenga Street hints at the traditional stone house behind its thick wooden door. A narrow passageway opens to a sun-filled courtyard, antique tiles set within the columns adding graceful colour to the whitewashed walls. In the traditional Swahili manner, outlying rooms on the ground floor are used for storage and day-to-day affairs and it is up the delicate wooden stairway that the family life of the house takes place. Once upstairs, a more private courtyard leads to separate apartments for the extended family to live, the open spaces made verdant with potted palms and ferns that lend it the atmosphere of an exotic garden.

Structurally, Indian stone houses differ from the traditional layout of a Swahili home by their use of wooden balconies instead of Arabian-inspired thick walls and small windows to cool the interior. Over time, balconies in Stone Town became status symbols in the Indian community and families vied with each other over their elaborateness and size. The Jafferji House reserves its use of balconies to the interior of the property, with finely carved wooden partitions shielding each floor from the direct light of the courtyards. Pillows covered in silk sari fabrics and elegant antique furniture adds a gracefully luxurious feel to light and breezy rooms that capture the magic of the Mughals and of Zanzibar, high above Stone Town's streets.

Left: A circle of candles adds sumptuous elegance to the oriental bath.

Left: Colourful cushions and hanging plants create a relaxing garden atmosphere off the upstairs courtyard. The small water tank to the right is traditionally used for washing hands before and after a meal.

Right: Swahili and Indian antiques line hardwood shelves that contrast gracefully with the bright white wall.

Left: An embroidered table runner from India accentuate bronze ornaments from Arabia and the Swahili Coast.
Right (clockwise from top left): An Omani dagger worn traditionally by Swahili aristocracy; a copper pot against a bright *mkeka* mat; an antique pitcher engraved with intricate designs; a dagger sheath against colourful Indian textiles.

The Palms

Stately villas in colonial style

On the far side of Zanzibar's east coast lies an exclusive property that effortlessly blends colonial grandeur with traditional design. Spacious verandas look out to sea as the unmistakable roaring of the outgoing tide carries over the water from the distant reef. Zanzibar's east coast is widely regarded as one of the best beaches in the world and The Palms takes every advantage of its superb vistas and seemingly endless horizon. The property is named after the hundreds of coconut palms that tower over the villas and drop their fruit on the thick grass daily. From the open windows of the spacious rooms, the rustling of their towering leaves is the first sound of the morning and the last one heard at night.

Each of the six spacious villas at The Palms was built with elegance in mind. Named after Zanzibar's spices and flowers, each one is a private world of stylish pampering and sophistication. Thick Swahili doors open onto a veranda complete with a private whirlpool and a four-poster Zanzibar bed, just for lounging. Inside, hardwood floors lead to rooms in earth tones of coffee and cream. A small table inlaid with handfuls of dried spices — cloves, cardamom, black peppercorns and cinnamon sticks — stands before a spacious and elegant sofa, while a canopied mosquito net surrounds a stately bed piled with billowing cushions. Old mirrors inlaid with hand-painted Indian tiles adorn the bedroom wall, where tall dark shutters open to palm trees and the ocean. In the bathroom, colourful bathrobes and dressing gowns made from traditional Swahili *kikois* hang beside the four-legged tub.

The common areas at The Palms are sophisticated manoeuvres in understated elegance. Vintage mirrors with gilded frames hang in front of a driftwood centrepiece, as a dozen old lanterns strung from its gnarled branches sway gently in the incoming breeze. The swimming pool floor is a mosaic of small blue tiles, each a different shade than the next, evocative of the grandeur of a Roman bath. Tall white planters' chairs line the shared veranda and face out to the ocean, perfect for socialising over well-mixed sundowners and enjoying vibrant sky. Inside, the art-deco bar is complemented by wooden ceiling fans and an antique chest of drawers. Stately furnishings in such tropical surroundings makes for a sometimes eclectic mix, but The Palms carries it off with grace and style.

Left: Private jacuzzis on each veranda add an element of romantic luxury to rooms at The Palms.

Left: Coffee and cream tones in the bedroom evoke chic safari living in tropical surroundings.
Right: Rooms at The Palms are a spacious and sedately stylish mix of neutral tones and gentle elegance.

Left: What better way to enjoy sunset than drinks for two on the beach.
Right: Private beach *bandas* make sure you get the very most out of sun-soaked days.

Left: Carved wooden borders and gauzy curtains make dining at The Palms an undeniably romantic experience.

Right: Beaded candle holders spread a soft glow throughout the room, where an attention to detail makes everything special.

Matemwe Bungalows
Hidden beaches and windswept coral cliffs

For over a decade now, Matemwe Bungalows has been one of the most treasured and secluded properties on Zanzibar Island. Tucked away in the quiet coves and bays of the northeast coast, Matemwe's fourteen bungalows are surrounded by lush tropical gardens and the wild expanses of the Indian Ocean. Tall groves of *mkadi* palms spread their finger-like roots high above the powdered sand, their thick fronds creating a sheltering canopy from the tropical sun. Sculpted succulents grown beneath them and hanging mobiles of driftwood, coral and shells sway from the branches of scented frangipani trees. Local birds flock to the property, where indigenous trees have been carefully planted to ensure that the delicately balanced habitat of the island remains intact.

Understated elegance is the foremost principle behind Matemwe's take on Swahili design and both the bungalows and the dining area are done in classic colours that emphasise the sand and sea. Each of the bungalows is perched atop a small outcrop of ancient coral, the rocks' stark edges framing expansive vistas of passing *ngalawa* fishing boats. The nearby reef lies close enough offshore for visitors to discern the figures of passing sailors and watch the flickering lanterns of night fishermen as they throw their nets under a shimmering cloak of stars. The muted colours of the bungalows and dining room match perfectly with the brilliant white of the beach's brilliant sand. In the flowering gardens, the skeleton of a whale that beached itself on the nearby reef has been reassembled with precision and care, its bleached bones evocative of the life and majesty of the bountiful ocean.

A key element of Matemwe's striking simplicity is its use of colour to evoke the surrounding environment. From the dining room, the beach and every bungalow, the reef and the vibrant waters of the Mnemba Atoll are visible in the distance. Embroidered appliqué bedspreads and cushions lend an oriental element to the thatched-roof bungalows, their dark blues and purples evoking the expansive ocean just outside. In the dining room, antique plates have been embedded into the walls in traditional Swahili style, their glazed colours complementing the bright array of pillows on the half-moon shaped *baraza*. From its view of the beach below, *kanga*-clad village women walk out to tide pools and returning fishermen moor their *dhows* in shallow waters, slowly carrying their heavy nets to shore.

Left: Embroidered cushions appliquéd in the Zanzibar style lend the romance of the spice islands to Matemwe's cottages.

Left: Matemwe's beachside bar was constructed from the hull of a retired sailing *dhow*.
Right: Up close, the *dhow* bar at Matemwe is a creative take on island style.

Swahili Doors

"Say to our brave men, 'Those who may come,
Will find our doors latched!'" Anonymous,

19th century Swahili poem

The exteriors of the Swahili Coast's stone houses are bare and unadorned, except for one feature – their doors. Large portals that open into cool and hidden courtyards of sunlight and small trees, they separate the public streets of old stone towns from the private world of sheltered domesticity inside. In Swahili culture, a door is as much a symbol of the wealth and status of the owner as it is a barrier between the outside world and the family's private life within. As the English explorer Richard Burton wrote in *Zanzibar*, "The higher the tenement, the bigger the gateway, the heavier the padlock and the huger the iron studs that nail the door of heavy timber, the greater is the owner's dignity."

Swahili doors are made exclusively of hardwood sourced in the forests of East Africa and although their carving styles and strucutures vary according to the residence and ethnic community of their owner, they are a common feature in Swahili towns from Mogadishu to Mozambique. Throughout the Islamic world carved doors were a sign of wealth and prosperity but only on the Swahili Coast, where craftsmen skilled in the knowledge of their construction had plentiful access to hardwood timber, were people able to afford them in such prolific numbers. Most of the carved doors in existence in Lamu, Mombasa and Zanzibar exhibit the common characteristics of a large door frame, a centre post and a lintel all carved in the geometric and floral motifs typical of Islamic decoration, sometimes inscribed with Qur'anic inscriptions and the date they were crafted.

Although the carved doors of the East African coast are commonly called 'Swahili,' their designs and structure differ greatly according to their style. Some specific types of carved doors include styles from Lamu, Siyu, Gujerat, Oman and Zanzibar – their structure, carving style and colourings varying vastly from one style to the next. Most doors in existence on the coast today date from the 19th century, when the Portuguese invaders were ousted by Omani forces and peace and prosperity returned to the East African coast. Although carved doors existed before that period, most would have deteriorated beyond repair by now. Many carved Swahili doors remain in use today throughout the old towns and settlements, ornate and beautiful relics of a bygone age.

Left: Most carved doors are still in use, as this Omani-style door in the street of the old town illustrates.
Right above: This semicircular lintel of a Zanzibar-style door is ornately carved with vines and a verse from the Qur'an.
Right below: Brass latches and door studs add to the ornateness of a Swahili carved door.

Dar es Salaam

"Bishop Tozer had a severe attack of fever, and I had persuaded him to accompany us for change of air, that of Darra Salaam being cool and refreshing. He returned with us at the end of a week quite another man."

G.L. Sulivan, *Dhow Chasing in Zanzibar Waters*

Dar es Salaam means 'haven of peace' in both Swahili and Arabic, and the prosperous commercial capital of Tanzania has strong roots in both Swahili and Arab history. A fairly recent addition to historical sites along the Swahili Coast, the location upon which the later city was founded remained a sleepy fishing village until the 1860's, when Sultan Sayyid Majid of Zanzibar chose the area's well-sheltered bay as an alternative harbour to the prosperous town of Bagamoyo further north. Shortly after, the sultan died and the small town soon slipped back into obscurity.

It was only in the late 1880's that the village of Dar es Salaam revived to become the bustling city it remains today. European missionaries used the harbour town as their first stop on the African mainland and trade slowly increased to the sheltered harbour. Richard Burton's expedition to find the source of the Nile departed from here, as did David Livingstone, Henry Stanley and many others who gradually brought the interior under the sway of European influence. In 1891, just a decade after Dar es Salaam's resurgence on the map of East African politics and trade, the German colonial administration officially moved their headquarters from Bagamoyo to Dar es Salaam and began the city's gradual increase in prosperity, trade and importance in the region.

Historical landmarks around Dar es Salaam place the it firmly within the Swahili tradition of culture and trade, but the city has more visible European colonial influences than many of its East African counterparts. Churches line the harbour's waterfront as a reminder of the city's Christian past – the Azania Front Lutheran Church and St. Joseph's Cathedral were both built by German missionaries in the early 1900's. The old German boma, for decades the administrative colonial centre of Tanganyika, still stands, now surrounded by the prosperous shops and office buildings of the business district. Today, tall buildings have grown around the old landmarks of Dar es Salaam, but above the traffic and urban sprawl of a populous African city, the cool winds that enticed Zanzibar's sultan still blow through the 'haven of peace.'

Left: Just south of the bustling city centre lie pristine beaches with hardly a person in sight.

Ras Kutani

Lagoon luxury in natural surroundings

I n Swahili, Ras Kutani means 'the meeting place,' a fitting name for a lodge whose natural environment is as conducive to romance and relaxation as it is for exploration and activity. Built around a lagoon created by the nearby Ngaramiko River, rooms face towards the water and reeds, where a narrow sandbank opens to the white-capped surf. Hundreds of birds, a cacophony of insects and many smaller species thrive around the banks of the lagoon as the Indian Ocean crashes just metres away. Although Ras Kutani is a mere hour from the urban bustle of Dar es Salaam, its atmosphere feels much more distant – the combination of natural environment, open-air lodging and untouched beach is as pristine and isolated as other more remote beach outposts.

The lodge's dining and sitting area combines space and privacy with traditional Swahili features, adding splashes of colour and detail to the natural environment. Blue and white *kangas* cover throw pillows and low seating, adding marine notes to otherwise neutral tones. The walls main area remain open to face both the lagoon and the ocean, all the better to catch the breeze and enjoy the play of sunlight on the sand and waves. Long wooden poles frame the corners to form dividing walls, their shapes fanned to resemble the rays of the sun. The sitting area consists of many small *baraza* angled to form private alcoves perfect socializing or a game of chess on classic wooden boards. An open deck faces the beach, where guests can sunbathe under bamboo shades or walk along a coastline fringed with palms and occasional baobab trees.

All of Ras Kutani's rooms face the water. On the verandas, deep blue hammocks are angled perfectly to face both the lagoon and the sea. Long wooden poles and woven *makuti* mats evoke the natural environment that surrounds the lodge and effortlessly blend the bungalow-style rooms with the trees and gardens outside. Gentle blue and white *kikoi* curtains filter the sunlight into golden shades. Outside, doum and borassus palms cover the grounds and create a sheltered atmosphere in contrast to the bright brilliance of the sand and sea. Each morning, the lagoon comes alive with birdlife as the sun gently seeps through the bungalows' open walls and windows. Come nightfall, canopies of mosquito netting envelop the bed to form soft white contours all the more splendid against the darkness outside.

Left: A quiet lagoon borders the rooms at Ras Kutani.

Left: Canvas hammocks hang from the verandas of each room, perfect for bird watching in the lagoon.
Right: Made almost entirely of local materials, the rooms at Ras Kutani feel close to nature.

Left: An *ngalawa* hull makes for a Swahili-style bar at the beach hut.
Right: Pillows covered in *kangas* add a Swahili element to the open-air sitting room.

Amani Beach Hotel

Arabian simplicity in Swahili gardens

Open space and plenty of light are paramount in environments where sun and the ocean play a large part in local style. Swahili architecture and design work elegantly to maximize comfort in the tropics, using archways, courtyards, screens and wall openings to channel breeze and let the sunshine in. Built with the philosophy of simplicity and classical style in mind, the Amani Beach Hotel is an exercise in Swahili style, its elements balanced to evoke the very peace and harmony for which the hotel is named. Located just an hour south of Dar es Salaam, the hotel has become a treasured retreat for city-dwellers and international guests alike.

Design elements and features from the Arabian Peninsula form the backbone of Amani Beach's style. The main building's exterior includes a row of archways from the dining room to the sitting and reception area, the garden and ocean visible through the open spaces. Antique lanterns sourced from the Egyptian bazaar in Cairo bring facets of the orient to the East African hotel. Engraved brass plates have been converted to stylish low tables and fluted copper urns hold potted palms. Hand-painted tiles from India have been converted into marble-topped tables, and Arabic calligraphy and hand-woven tapestries hang from the walls, all collected by the property's owners during their travels around Africa and the Middle East. The use of antiques and traditional architecture evokes the blend of African and Arab styles that characterizes Swahili design.

Gardens also play an important part in creating the relaxed atmosphere at Amani Beach, providing a natural haven ideal for rest and rejuvenation. Thick leaved haliconia, flamboyant trees, frangipani and flourishes of multi-coloured bougainvillea bring colour and shade to the expansive lawns. Mango trees and yellow oleander add a tropical element to gardens perpetually cooled by the ocean breeze. The hotel's swimming pool looks out over the beach, a small bar and shaded seating area perfect for cooling off or lounging the day away with a good book. Despite the hotel's proximity to Dar es Salaam, the property's beach is completely private and secluded. Along the shore, large rocks and high cliffs create a dramatic backdrop to the Indian Ocean, the nearby hills covered with palms and scattered baobabs, bringing the wilderness of the bush to a perfect beach.

Left: Low chairs encircle a coffee table styled around an engraved copper plate, invoking the Arabian elements of Amani's style.

Left: Elaborate Arabic calligraphy continue the traditional Swahili theme.
Right: Hand-woven textiles from North Africa recall the close ties between the Swahili Coast and the Arab world.

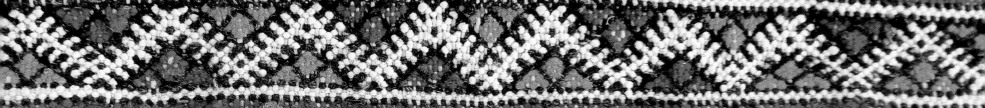

Traditional Dress

"Happy, pleased-looking men with long white cotton shirts move about with quick, active motion and cry out to their friends or mates in the Swahili or Arabic language."

Henry Stanley, *Through the Dark Continent*

The Swahili way of life is based both around both the dictates of Islam and the tropical environment of the East African coast. The body must be protected from high, humid temperatures and blustering monsoon winds while remaining covered in a modest, conservative style. In the city-states and sultanates of the coast's golden age, traditional dress signified high social standing and lavish ceremonial costumes remained the privilege of the wealthy merchant and aristocratic classes. Slaves wore simple wraps, purely functional clothing for performing their duties.

Public dress conceals and veils a Swahili woman's face, body and hair from the gaze of strangers. Once inside the privacy of her own home or the *harem* women's quarters of friends or relatives, she is permitted to unveil. Traditional Swahili women only venture out in public cloaked in the head-to-toe black of a *bui bui* or *shuga*. In the past, rich women would wear a veil to fully cover their eyes and advance down the street guided by slaves who called out to the men on the street to turn away until the woman had passed. Once safely protected from the public gaze, the *bui bui* would be discarded to reveal elaborately embroidered and coloured dresses, tunics and loose trousers in the Indian and Omani style. Working women wear the traditional two-piece *kanga* day and night, its versatile shape easily wrapped into a variety of coverings and styles.

Men's dress has more ceremonial connotations and makes a public statement about the wealth and social standing of the wearer. Traditional Swahili dress comprised a *kitakatea*, a thin cotton undershirt and a *kikoi*, a wraparound cloth traditionally hand-woven in Somalia. A white embroidered hat called a *kofia* is worn in public, its design often indicating where a man is from. Traditional Islamic dress is based around the *kanzu*, a long white robe worn with a *kikoi* and *kitakatea* underneath. A *kilemba*, or a silk turban, may be wrapped around the *kofia* and a *sheikh* or religious leader would also wear a *kizibao*, or dark vest. A long dark woolen robe called a *joho* and a ceremonial dagger tied with a *mahazamu*, or a silk sash, completes the costume for ceremonial occasions.

Left: A fisherman in his dugout *mashua* wears a simple shirt and a traditional striped *kikoi*.
Right: Women cloaked in the head-to-toe black of the Swahili *bui-bui* covering walk down a street in Lamu Town.

Mafia Island

"The island is small, near the mainland, and is a beautiful country. In this land there are rich merchants, and there is much gold and silver and amber and musk and pearls."

Duarte Barbarosa, 1517

Twenty kilometres east of Tanzania's Rufiji River Delta, as the sea turns a darker blue amidst atolls and sandbars, is the island and small archipelago of Mafia. An ancient trading port allied with the better-known Kilwa Kisiwani further south, Mafia's capital of Kisimani was home to sailors and traders from all over the Indian Ocean, men who voyaged bravely on the open seas and married local women for seasonal sweethearts, returning to their Swahili homes with the advent of the changing winds. Wealthy merchants owned large plantations on the larger island of Mafia, where slaves from central Africa lived and laboured in the coconut groves that were the island's chief export to the outside world.

To protect themselves from occasional invaders and the slave uprisings that were common on Mafia plantations, the Swahili aristocracy chose the smaller island of Chole Mjini as their domain. Situated a few hundred metres from the larger island's shores, Chole became the retreat for the ruling classes of Mafia. Large houses and shops hewn from kiln-baked coral lined the shoreline and a small port was cleared from the thick mangrove forests that enveloped the island. Basking in the verdant fertility of their tropical isle, the wealthy merchants planted large gardens of flowers and groves of fruit trees brought from across the ocean. Old trunks of pomegranates and oranges planted by the slave traders continue to flourish on the island. Groves of citron, cashews, mangoes, guavas, lemons and tamarind trees still scent the breeze with memories of a vanished past.

These days, the islands are home to a thriving population of fruit bats, whose furry yellow bodies and vampire wings can be seen hanging from high trees during the day. In the evening, the bats take flight in an eerie display of striking magnificence as bushbabies rustle and call high in the abandoned branches. Deep underwater, the coral reefs of Mafia offer some of the best diving in the region. Pristine, protected and little visited, sea turtles, dolphins and even the occasional humpbacked whale have made the archipelago their home. From the shadow of slave traders and their plantations has blossomed a veritable island paradise, with hardly a footprint on the shore.

Left: The ruins of Chole Mjini were once a prosperous Swahili town of plantation owners and merchants.

Kinasi Lodge

Eclectic elegance on a secluded island

K inasi stands high on a hilltop, overlooking the secluded Chole Bay on the south-eastern side of Mafia Island. Sandy pathways and artfully curving steps edged with wave patterns lead down to a private beach shaded by coconut palms and native trees that stretch across the lawns. Islands small and large stretch green against the horizon, their shores just visible through the haze. From each of Kinasi's twelve cottages, the ocean appears in snatches between rustling palm fronds, frangipani canopies and native *Albizzia* trees. From each cottage's generous veranda the sparkling water appears to be floating at arm's length.

Owners Antonella Balestra and Peter Byrne have created a stylish resort from a unique blend of Arab, Indian and African designs, furniture, fabrics and their personal collectables. Fabrics from Italy and Spain add elegance and elevate the quality of finish. Mafia itself has provided some beautiful and unexpected antiques over the years. The style Antonella and Peter call *Shirazi* reflects the variety of influences that have created the designs of buildings, furniture and ornament seen throughout the Stone Town of Zanzibar, Lamu, old Mombasa, Kilwa and other historic ports. Mafia — once a satellite of the all-powerful trade depot of Kilwa — played a role in this history and has historic sites and buildings from the golden age of Indian Ocean trade.

Moroccan antique candle lanterns and lampshades bestow a special magic on Kinasi after nightfall. Splinters of light fall through coloured glass as hundreds of small shadows, the shape of flower petals and ragged diamonds, infuse the flavour of the Maghreb into this hideaway property.

Each room is named after an Indian Ocean island and decorated in a particular style — the India room's glittering mirrors and canopied silk saris make it a particular favourite.

Kinasi is designed for guests to take pleasure in every moment spent under the tropical sun and a full programme of activities such as diving and snorkelling and well-organised excursions to villages, historical sites, forests, isolated beaches and islets ensure that visitors enjoy a full experience. Antonella and Peter call this the "*Mafia Immersion*" ; there is a great sense of family and fun at Kinasi, with its very friendly staff, and as a result referral and repeat business is now Kinasi's most important source of guests.

The gardens are wide and spacious, full of meandering paths that lead up and down the sun-drenched hills, with generous concessions to sea and sky. Down at the beach, beds and shaded hammocks are spaced discreetly between shade trees for privacy. Swimming in the gentle waves of high tide, the water is warm and inviting. Everything at Kinasi is airy and uninhibited, as if the island itself exists only for you. Navy hammocks swing beneath the bungalows' thatched roofs and towards nightfall the bungalow walls, already painted a luxurious deep yellow, glow golden in the last rays of the setting sun.

Left: The muted earth tones of the lodge evoke the fecundity of lush green surroundings.

Left: Carved doorways and Moroccan furniture create an oriental ambience inside
the main area.
Right: Open windows and plenty of colour add to the ambience of the dining room.

Left: Rope pulleys used on old *dhow* boats, baskets and boxes add detail to the main area.

Right: Porthole windows and high-backed stools add nautical accents to the bar area.

Left: High *baraza* sitting areas and Arab lanterns completes the meeting of Swahili and Arabian design elements.

Right: A high bed inset with antique plates creates a delicate Swahili ambience in the rooms.

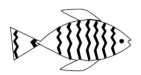

Chole Mjini

Treetop living above time-worn ruins

Chole Mjini is something unique in an ocean of lodges that boast beautiful vistas and exceptional rooms. Its seven bungalows are built entirely in the treetops above the tumbling ruins of an old Arab port. Narrow stairways rise to two-level cottages perched against ancient baobabs and flamboyant trees. Large sofas with generous cushions stand against woven thatch walls. Everything is made from natural materials, as if the lodge itself grew out of the abandoned forest. The tree house bungalows shadow the derelict houses of Arab merchants and Indian shopkeepers, the old walls ravaged by thick strangler figs as they slowly give way to time. The sounds of lapping waves caressing the mangrove thickets at high tide rise clearly to open-air balconies where sunset becomes a private occasion high in the island canopy.

At Chole Mjini, everything is improvised and invented. By the dressing-room table, coconut ladles of fresh water stand beneath an upturned mirror as *dhow* masts and flapping sails bob gently in the nearby waters, their silhouettes just visible through the coconut rope walls. Hand-dyed fabrics in indigos and blue canopy large beds strewn with frangipani flowers. A sun-bleached sail cloth shades the balconies outside and coconut rope, strung in tightly parallel segments and interspersed with woven palm mats, covers the back side of each tree house. The rest lies entirely open to the warm wind and sea, the dawn breeze caressesing the curtains as the first rays of sun slant into the bedroom. Hanging beds rock gently back and forth, suspended from mangrove poles while the leathery trunks of old baobabs stand sentinel in the corner. A turret balcony rises above each elevated room for a bird's-eye view of the island and the archipelago beyond.

The atmosphere of the lodge is one of timelessness-the feeling of being inside history, of a forgotten world that hasn't changed in the century after its desertion. The only way to arrive in Chole Mjini is by *dhow* from the island of Mafia, but even that short journey seems to span centuries. Dinner is served barefoot in the ruins of an Arab merchant's house, hurricane lanterns strung by the dozen from vines and branches. When the sun rises above glistening islands to turn the sea a soft silver, attendants leave trays of tea at the bottom of the stairs for a private sunrise high in the baobab trees.

Left: Canopied mosquito nets and a naturally printed bedspread add to the open-air effect of Chole Mjini's tree houses.

Left: Up high against the trunk of an ancient baobab tree, this tree houses afford a bird's eye view of the archipelago and the ocean.
Right: Made completely from natural materials, each of the tree houses are different in subtle ways.

Left: The view of a gnarled baobab trunk through the open window is a striking reminder that you're in Africa.

Right: Nature is high on the priority list at Chole Mjini as this baobab trunk, a central feature of the tree house, clearly shows.

Left: The deck area of Chole Mjini is ideal for relaxing and soaking up the natural surroundings.
Right (clockwise from top left): Wash stands and woven *mkeka* baskets in the treetops; a lounge bed with a view; even the showers are an all-natural experience; woven coconut rope creates textured walls in the tree houses.

Mkeka and Makuti

"In Chole there are picturesque huts close to pomegranate and orange trees on the verandas of which sit women, skilfully plaiting their mats. In the fields are scattered many houses, all of which have yards walled with *mtwara* straw."

Arab trader in Mafia, 19th century

Natural materials have always played an important part in the designs and styles of the Swahili Coast. For hundreds of years, local trade in woven mats and coconut rope supported a bustling industry for village women, who created unique styles and weaving techniques. Rectangular mats called *mkeka* line the floor of houses, woven mats called *misala* are used five times a day for the Muslim prayer and hat-shaped funnels called *mahawa* cover dishes of food to ward off the flies. Wealthy Arab merchants lined the floors of their *harems* with colourful mats and during the German occupation of Mafia, export of *mkeka* was second only to coconuts. Palm trees continue to provide the bulk of raw materials for weaving – everything from thatched *makuti* roofs to woven floor mats, all as much in use today as they were in the heyday of the Arab sultans.

Chole, a small island off the larger land mass of Mafia, has been the centre of the fibre trade on the Swahili Coast since the 10th century. Unique designs and colourful patterns have always been a part of the craft, with buyers choosing from styles like 'gecko's spine,' 'fish trap,' 'crow's wing,' and even 'popcorn' for their mats and coverings. To add colour to the mats, thin strips of dried palm fronds are dyed in indigenous roots, leaves and fruits, although over the years Indian merchants have done a bustling trade in more eye-catching hues. The coloured strips are woven into one-centimetre lengths, then sewn together into a larger piece and finished with a solid border.

Thatched roofs called *makuti* are also popular throughout the Swahili Coast. Bundles of dried palm fronds are tied tightly to the beams of a sloping roof – their waxy coating makes them naturally waterproof when the monsoon rains arrive. Every few seasons, the roofs are replaced by hand. Even after centuries, the importance of weaving in the daily lives of women on Mafia hasn't changed. To this day, women weave and talk in the evening sun, plaiting colourful mats and baskets for export to the mainland of East Africa and beyond.

Left: A woman in Mafia plaits *mkeka* mats by hand.
Right: Woven *mkeka*, in its many colours and styles, can be used for a variety of items.

Glossary

afrit – another word for jinn or *sheitani*; malicious or harmful spirits

banda – a small cottage or hut

baraza – stone benches that form outcrops against a wall or street, used as public meeting places by Swahili men

boma – an open enclosure, also a fort-like centre of colonial administration

bui bui – the black robes and veil Swahili women wear in public

daka – the porch before the carved door or entrance to a stone house, often with steps and a nearby *baraza*

dhow – a wooden fishing or cargo boat powered by sail and made of mangrove and other wood *fundi* – a craftsman

furungu – heavy anklets of silver or gold that made traditional dowry gifts, often in pairs, with small dangling chains

gali – knives with handles made of hippo tooth ivory and often inlaid with gold

hajj – the annual pilgrimage to Mecca, a once-in-a-lifetime obligation under Islamic law to those who can afford it

hamaam – a public or private bathhouse in the traditional Arab or Turkish style

jahazi – the largest kind of sailing boat used to transport cargo across the Indian Ocean

jambia – Omani-style daggers made by silversmiths around the Swahili Coast

jinn – invisible spirits, whom one can placate, ward off or expel

kanga – a pair of printed cotton cloths worn by women in East Africa; printed cotton with a multicoloured border, a pattern and a proverb

kanzu – a white robe worn by Swahili men, often ceremonial

kijani – green; new growth, new life; the colour of Islam

kitakatea – a thin cotton undershirt worn with a *kikoi*

kikoi – a long cloth of woven cotton in various colours with horizontal stripes, worn as part of traditional Swahili dress, hand-woven in Somalia

kisu cha kisiyu – a traditional knife made on the island of Siyu

kitenge – thick printed cloth that comes in rolls, usually sewn into dresses for women

kiwanda – the first floor courtyard of a traditional Swahili stone house

kofia – a white pillbox-type hat worn by Muslim men on the coast, embroidered in different designs depending on its place of origin

kuba – West African textiles hand-woven with natural materials

leso – printed cotton kerchiefs or bandanas

liwali – local ministers serving under the sultan

mahawa – hat-shaped funnels of woven palm fronds used to cover dishes of food to keep away flies

majasi – decorative earplugs worn by women, made of silver, gold, or animal horn

makuti – woven coconut palm thatch tied to mangrove poles, the traditional roofs of Swahili houses

makowa – long bracelets that clasp around the forearm and come in pairs

mangati – long wooden poles that form the roof beams of traditional stone houses

marekani – thin cotton cloth in plain colours, usually white or cream

mashrabeya – intricate and hand carved Arab lattice-work made from hard wood and screwed together without adhesive; *mashrabeya* balconies and windows traditionally allowed female residents of the house a view of the streets below without being seen

matamvuwe – the hand-twisted fringe at either end of a *kikoi*

mdaba – a shaded sitting area on the outside of a stone house reserved for male visitors

mihrab – the central focus of a mosque, an embedded niche that indicates the direction towards Mecca

misala – woven palm frond mats used for the Muslim prayer

miwandi – a long round pole built into the wall of an upstairs bedroom from which a curtain was hung to provide privacy

mkeka – woven sisal or palm frond mats of rectangular shape in a variety of patterns and colours

mtaa – neighbourhoods of stone houses in old Swahili towns

msana wa tini – the second floor veranda that overlooks the courtyard of a stone house

muezzin – the Muslim cleric responsible for sounding the call to prayer

ngalawa – the smallest of Swahili boats, a wooden catamaran used for fishing

niru – a Lamu technique of working on cement and plaster that varies the colour and texture of the flat surface

ntazanyao – the small wooden stool used to reach high Swahili carved beds

nyumba – house

pavilao – high four-poster beds made of hardwood and ornately carved, sometimes with Indian painted tiles inset into the headboard and footboard

konde – plantations owned by Swahili merchants where food was grown to feed the family and its retainers in town

kuba – West African cloth made from natural materials in geometric patterns

sheitani – ghosts or devils

shuga – a black cloak worn by women when in public, similar to a *bui bui*

taarab – a traditional genre of Swahili music originally based upon the songs of slaves yearning for freedom; *taraab* music has been profoundly influenced by the drumming styles of Egypt and the Arab world, where many of its founding musicians studied

tambu ya uraibu – a holder for snuff made from betel nut and tobacco, wrapped in a *tambu* leaf

Tinga-tinga – a colourful style of painting animals and village scenes pioneered in Dar es Salaam by Edward Saidi Tinga-tinga and now popular throughout the East African coast

tirazi – the woven band at the end of a *kikoi*

uipete – a series of small earrings worn by women along their earlobes

ute – the technique of using string instead of wicker to back a bed or wooden chair

viyatu – shoes

viyatu vya kutoma – leather sandals for women, traditionally made on the island of Siyu in the Lamu Archipelago

viyatu vya maku badhi – leather sandals for men, traditionally made on the island of Siyu in the Lamu Archipelago

zidaka – small alcoves and niches found in a Swahili house, originally intended for storing things

---

Left: A builder quarries limestone blocks from the shore of Matondoni on Lamu Island.

Contact Addresses

LAMU
Baytil Ajaib
P.O. Box 328
Lamu, Kenya
Tel (254) 42 632033
mail@baytilajaib.com
www.baytilajaib.com
www.chicretreats.com

Beach House
P.O. Box 39486
Nairobi 00623, Kenya
Tel (254) 20 4442171
Fax (254) 20 4445010
shela@africaonline.co.ke
www.lamu-shela.com or www.shelahouse.com

Johari House
P.O. Box 86
Karen 00502, Kenya

Kijani House Hotel
P.O. Box 266
Lamu, Kenya
Tel (254) 42 633235/6/7 or 733 616231
Fax (254) 42 633374
kijani@africaonline.co.ke
www.kijani-house.com

Kipungani Explorer
Heritage Management Limited
P.O. Box 74888
00200 Nairobi Kenya
Tel (254) 20 4446651 or 4447929
Fax (254) 20 4446600 or 4446533
sales@heritagehotels.co.ke
www.heritage-eastafrica.com

Moon Houses
Tel (33) 1 42229266 or
(33) 6 15931072
spoerry@noos.fr or anitaspoerry@mac.com
vanishingafrica@hotmail.com

Munira's Island Camp
P.O. Box 40088
Nairobi 00100, Kenya
Tel (254) 20 512213 or 733 583627/963813
Fax (254) 20 512543

bigblue@africaonline.co.ke
www.kiwayuisland.com

Peponi Hotel
P.O. Box 24
Lamu 80500, Kenya
Tel (254) 42 633421/3/4 or 633154
Mobile (254) 722 203082 or 734 203082
Fax (254) 42 633029
peponi@africaonline.co.ke
www.peponi-lamu.com

Shela and Palm House
P.O. Box 39486
Nairobi 00623, Kenya
Tel (254) 20 4442171
Fax (254) 20 4445010
shela@africaonline.co.ke
www.lamu-shela.com or www.shelahouse.com

Tusitiri Dhow
P.O. Box 24498
Nairobi 00502, Kenya
Tel (254) 733 649833
tusitiridhow@africaonline.co.ke

MOMBASA
Alfajiri Villas
P.O. Box 454
Ukinda, Kenya
Tel (254) 40 3202630
Fax (254) 40 3202218
molinaro@africaonline.co.ke
www.alfajirivillas.com

The Funzi Keys
International Reservations
Orion Park
Northfield Avenue
London W13 9SJ, United Kingdom
Tel (44) 20 8840 2900
Fax (44) 20 8840 2950
funzikeys@aboutafrica.co.uk
www.thefunzikeys.com

Serena Beach Hotel
P.O. Box 90352
Mombasa, Kenya
Tel (254) 41 5485721/2/3
Fax (254) 41 5485453
mombasa@serena.co.ke
www.serenahotels.com

ZANZIBAR
Emerson & Green Hotel
P.O. Box 3417
Zanzibar, Tanzania
Tel (255) 747 423266
Fax (255) 747 429266
emerson&green@zitec.org
www.emerson-green.com

Matemwe Bungalows
P.O. Box 3275
Zanzibar, Tanzania
Tel (255) 747 425788
Fax (255) 747 429788
info@matemwe.com
www.matemwe.com

The Palms
P.O. Box 1361
Zanzibar, Tanzania
Tel (255) 747 415049
Fax (255) 741 333151
thepalms@africaonline.co.tz
info@palms-zanzibar.com
www.palms-zanzibar.com

Zanzibar Serena Inn
P.O. Box 4151
Zanzibar, Tanzania
Tel (255) 24 2233587
Fax (255) 24 2233019
zserena@zanzinet.com
www.serenahotels.com

DAR ES SALAAM
Protea Amani Beach Hotel
P.O. Box 1736
Dar es Salaam, Tanzania
Tel (255) 744 410033
Fax (255) 22 2667760
proteaamani@africaonline.co.tz

www.proteahotels.com/amani
www.amanibeach.com

Ras Kutani
Box 1192 Dar es Salaam, Tanzania
Tel: (255) 22 2134794
Fax: (255) 22 2112794
info@selous.com
www.selous.com

MAFIA
Chole Mjini
2chole@bushmail.net
cholemjini@africatravelresource.com

Kinasi Lodge
P.O. Box 18033
Dar es Salaam, Tanzania
Tel (255) 741 324463 or 744 481033
Fax (255) 24 2238220
kinasi@zanlink.com
www.mafiaisland.com

The following airlines provide internal flights within Tanzania and Kenya.

Air Kenya
P.O. Box 30357, Nairobi, Kenya
Tel (254) 20 601727 or 601734
Fax (254) 20 602951
resvns@airkenya.com
www.airkenya.com

Coastal Travels Ltd.
P.O. Box 3052
Dar es Salaam, Tanzania
Tel (255) 22 2117959/60
Mobile (255) 744 324044 or 744 325673
Fax (255) 22 2118647
safari@coastal.cc
www.coastal.cc

Left: A *marimba*, a traditional Swahili muscial instrument made from local materials.

Acknowledgments

This book spans two countries, many trips and a singular vision. Although it's impossible to include everyone who has inspired
and assisted us along the way, a very special thank-you goes out to the following:
From the Nairobi side, thanks to Catherine Kamau and everyone at Air Kenya for supporting the project.
In Lamu, many thanks to Lars and Carol Korschen at Peponi for their boundless hospitality, Pierre and Mwananshee Oberson of Kijani for their wealth
of historical and cultural knowledge and guidance, Peter and Mike Kennedy and Cinda Rumbold for making Kiwayu happen in such a magical way, Paul
Weaver and Norbert Herget at Baytil Ajaib for their continued support, Leslie Duckworth and Angelika Schuetz of Shela, Palm and Beach House, Bernard and
Anita Spoerry of the Moon Houses, George Kariuki in Heritage office and Eric at Kipungani, Mark and
Richenda Eddy on Tusitiri Dhow and Allan and Moyra Earnshaw of Johari House.
In Mombasa, many thanks to Mugo Maringa for us support of the project from start to finish, Fabrizio and Marika Molinaro
and Alessandro and Claudia Torriani.
Along the Tanzanian coast, thanks to Peter and Antonella Byrnes and Anne and Jean de Villiers on Mafia and Lyn Balkwill at Ras Kutani.
In Zanzibar, thanks to Nathalie Raguz Fusillo, Adriano Fusillo, Paulina Raguz and Aaren Macksoud at The Palms, Charles Muia at the Zanzibar Serena
Inn and Lena Horlin, Alastair Norton-Griffiths and Jane Oxborrow at Matemwe.
A special thanks to Ibrahim Khutri at Protea Amani Beach Hotel and Kulsum Jafferji to being so patient on the road and to Abid and Bashira Jafferji for all the
encoragement in life and to Maarten Boeye for his unconditional support and encouragement.

Sources

Aldrick, Judith. 'The Nineteenth-Century Carved Wooden Doors of the East African Coast.' Azania: The Journal of the British Institute in Eastern Africa. Vol 25.
1990.

Battuta, Ibn. "A Visit to Zeila, Mogadishu, Mombasa, and Kilwa Kisiwani in 1331." *The East African Coast: Select Documents from the First to the Earlier Nineteenth
Century*. Ed. Stewart Greenville and Parker Freeman. Oxford: Clarendon Press, 1962.

Burton, Richard. Zanzibar: City, Island and Coast. London: 1872.

Da Gama, Vasco. "The Discovery of East Africa for Portugal, 1498." *The East African Coast: Select Documents from the First to the Earlier Nineteenth Century*. Ed.
Stewart Greenville and Parker Freeman. Oxford: Clarendon Press, 1962.

Ghaidan, Usam. *Lamu: A Study of the Swahili Town*. Nairobi: Kenya Literature Bureau, 1992.

McCrae, J. *The Old Town of Mombasa: A Historical Guide*. Ed. J. Aldrick, R. Macdonald and J. Maitland-Hones. Mombasa: The Friends of Fort Jesus, 1997.

Mwinyi Bahari, Mtoro bin. Plasterwork and Doors: The Customs of the Swahili People. Ed. and trans. J. Allen. Berkekley: UC Press, 1974.

Nurse, Derek and Thomas Spear. *The Swahili: Reconstructing the History and Language of an African Society, 800-1500*. Philadelphia: University of Pennsylvania Press,
1985.

Stanley, Henry. *Through the Dark Continent*. New York: Harper and Brothers, 1879

Sulivan, G.L. *Dhow Chasing in Zanzibar Waters and on the Eastern Coast of Africa*. London: Frank Cass and Co. Ltd., 1901.

Vizetelly, Edward. *From Cypus to Zanzibar by the Egyptian Delta: The Adventures of a Journalist in the Isle of Love, the Home of Miracles, and the Land of Cloves*. London:
C. Arthur Pearson Ltd., 1901